WHAT ⌐
ARE YOU?

Sneha Shah is a consulting psychologist with a double major in psychology. She has trained over 75,000 people in the last ten years and offers webinars that are attended by a global audience. She has presented workshops in ten countries and her work has been translated into six international languages. She is certified in several psychometric tools and assessments, including Emotional Intelligence Profiling, FIRO-B, MBTI, Psycho-Geometrics®, Action Centered Leadership, Coach U and Enneagram. She is one of the few certified Teacher Trainers for Heal Your Life® USA, and is also one of the few professionals in India to practice the Gottman Couples Therapy Method.

Dr Susan Dellinger is creator of the Psycho-Geometrics® system of analysing personal communication styles. Since the inception of this system in 1978, Dr Dellinger has presented her unique system to over one million people in 24 countries.

Praise for *What Shape Are You?*

'Beware, you are about to change the way you see relationships forever. Explained through stories, Sneha will make the art of understanding people easy. You will apply what you learn immediately and this will change your life. You have been warned!'

—Fernando Niño, author, Founder and Gerente
General of Grupo Macro (Ecuador)

'*What Shape Are You?* is one of the most relatable books I have read in recent times, and this will hold true for everyone who reads it! The premise of using shapes to understand yourself and those you love is simple, yet deeply profound. Kudos to Sneha Shah—the subject matter, anecdotes and straight-from-the-heart writing style make this book a must-read!'

—Lucia Giovannini, best-seller author and
spiritual teacher (Italy)

'Sneha's book is a brilliant presentation of a rather simple, yet especially comprehensive framework for understanding personality differences in oneself and others, which can then be readily applied to dramatically improve your relationships at home and at work. By knowing the key personality attributes of five geometric shapes (i.e., a box, triangle, circle, rectangle and a squiggle), anyone can quickly learn the inherent beauty (strengths) and unique challenges (shortcomings) of making primary use of one geometric shape or another. But by consciously knowing these personality differences in oneself and others, everyone can be encouraged to develop a much more balanced approach to personality differences in their life by learning when to use the key attributes of each personality shape in a more productive and satisfying manner. This book will help you communicate more effectively with others by explicitly taking those different shapes (lenses) of personality into account. Engaging in radically improved communication will then make it much easier for you to resolve the constant stream of conflicts that always arise from personality differences. Bottom line: by applying the key principles in Sneha's book, more people will get their most important needs met, which will generate greater health, happiness and long-term organisational success throughout the world.'

—Ralph H. Kilmann, PhD, co-author of the Thomas–Kilmann
Conflict-Mode Instrument (TKI) and CEO, Kilmann Diagnostics
(www.kilmanndiagnostics.com) (USA)

'I was amazed to see how this practical, easy-to-use tool could provide deep insights into self-awareness and how we relate to people. This beautiful book reflects Sneha Shah's engaging style and years of experience. It provides a guide for everyone to apply throughout their lives. Imagine the difference we could make in the world if we had a deeper insight about ourselves and the people around us. I truly believe this is the greater purpose of Sneha's work.'

—Aylin Algun, MA in Applied Psychology, author of *Heal Your Life*, and Teacher-Coach, Corporate Trainer and Academic Associate in Viktor Frankl's Logotherapy (Turkey)

'If you think no man is an island, this book is for you. It treasures all the a-ha moments you'll ever need to release your painful struggle to fit your nearest and dearest into the moulds you created for them when you thought you were just loving them. Or to make your boss offer you a promotion with the highest possible bonuses. And that's just the tip of the iceberg! Dare to dive in, grab your a-ha moments and emerge as your best you!'

—Ivana Tomic (Serbia)

'Bible scripture admonishes us to love our neighbour as ourselves. That's all well and good. In fact, I believe it is ultimately the key to world peace. However, the continuing reality is that many neighbours are difficult to love or even like! *What Shape Are You?* by Sneha Shah offers us a pathway to learning to love ourselves and our neighbours by understanding personality traits as they relate to specific geometric shapes. Sneha's gracious presentation of these materials offers a delightful way to learn how to bring more peace to yourself, your family, the workplace and indeed the world at large. So, no matter the shape you find yourself in, you have much to gain from the revelations in this book. Enjoy!'

—Rick Nichols, award-winning author of *Love Will Lead Us Home: Your Guide for the Journey* and *Who Do You Think You Are? A Fairy Tale for All Ages* (USA)

'In a modern world with so many differences between individuals, this incredible book in a completely new way "shapes" our attitudes about ourselves, other people and life generally. Sneha Shah uses her decade-long knowledge in the field of human behaviour and gives us fantastic opportunities to understand, heal and improve our relationships using the simple but very powerful tools described in this book. *What Shape Are You?* is a must-read for those who want to live a meaningful and prosperous life.'

—Sinisa Ubovic (Serbia)

'We have all asked the question: Why does my spouse, friend, parent or co-worker think and act so differently from me? The revelations in this book will have you nodding, agreeing and perhaps even laughing as you read the characteristics of different personalities based on the shapes of a box, triangle, circle, rectangle and squiggle and relate them to people in your life. Author Sneha Shah offers many stories illustrating the attributes of the different shapes along with how to effectively communicate with them, and strategies to support them and yourself. *What Shape Are You?* is a powerful guide for living life more harmoniously with yourself and others. Read it—you will definitely gain benefits from this method for enhanced human understanding.'

—Patricia J. Crane, PhD, best-selling author of
Ordering from the Cosmic Kitchen, trainer and speaker (USA)

SNEHA SHAH
DR SUSAN DELLINGER

WHAT
SHAPE
ARE
YOU?

Discover Who You Really Are
& How to Handle Everyone
Who Isn't Like You

First published by Westland Books, a division of Nasadiya Technologies Private Limited, in 2023

No. 269/2B, First Floor, 'Irai Arul', Vimalraj Street, Nethaji Nagar, Allappakkam Main Road, Maduravoyal, Chennai 600095

Westland and the Westland logo are the trademarks of Nasadiya Technologies Private Limited, or its affiliates.

ISBN: 9789395767873

10 9 8 7 6 5 4 3 2 1

The views and opinions expressed in this work are the authors' own and the facts are as reported by them, and the publisher is in no way liable for the same.

Fictitious names have been used for clients to protect their identity.

Typeset by SÜRYA, New Delhi

Printed at Nutech Print Services-India

Shashank, this book is a result of your belief in me.
You truly are the wind beneath my wings.

CONTENTS

1

'Why Are You Like This?'

One afternoon, sitting at my favourite café with a cup of steaming coffee in my hand, I was having a conversation with this love-struck to-be-married friend. The dreamy look in her eyes, the goofy grin plastered on her face, eyes alight, skin glowing, she looked completely in love. 'He is everything I have always dreamt of,' she gushed. Intrigued, I asked her what she meant by that.

'He makes me feel so complete. He is everything that I am not,' she said with a faraway look in her eyes. 'In what way?' I asked a little sceptically. 'He is strong, ambitious, confident and speaks his mind so clearly. He is so assured and at ease with people. I love that about him. It's almost as if my life has expanded after I met him. He is so full of energy, and there's not a dull moment with him,' she replied.

I reflected on what she had said and realised it was true. My otherwise soft, docile, sensitive friend, who had always been extremely selective about who she befriended or went out with, did seem vibrant and full of life.

Three years later, back in the same café with a steaming cup of coffee in my hand, this very friend of mine tells me she cannot stand the sight of the man she was once so head over heels in love with.

'What happened?' I ask her gently. 'He is so stubborn and aggressive. He has to get his bloody way at everything. He is an insensitive and selfish a**hole. I just can't stand being with him anymore,' she answers with tears in her eyes. The fairy-tale romance has turned into a nightmare. While he has not really changed as a person, she now sees a different side of him. Rather, the same side, but differently.

I have seen many versions of this in my career, and it amazes me every single time how extroverts find themselves drawn to the quiet introverts, how high achievers can be attracted to the relaxed and laid-back ones, how partygoers find themselves with solitude-seekers and the impulsive spenders gravitate towards the practical and thrifty savers.

What seems like the perfect example of two halves creating a whole doesn't always remain harmonious. The very things that seemed attractive, intriguing and different in the beginning now start to become a thorn in the side—prickly, irritating, offensive.

Let's get to the root of it. Human relationships are governed by the law of complementarity. We get attracted to people whose personality complements or fits with ours to create a more complete or whole system. Each provides a counterbalance to the other. Why? Because this prevents the relationship from becoming unstable and moving towards one extreme or another. Makes sense, doesn't it?

This happens to be true not only in intimate relationships but also with friends, family, colleagues and siblings. These differences in personality allow us to build a different perspective—to share strengths, to balance weaknesses and to solve issues that we can't solve alone. This helps us grow as individuals.

That's exactly what my ambitious, extroverted, well-networked, 'life of the party' sister does. She offers the perfect contrast to my sensitive, overly thoughtful, introverted perspective on life. Often, when I get caught up with the smaller issues, she reminds me to stop being a victim and take charge of my life. Sometimes, that is exactly the whack I need on my head.

Whether personal, professional or social, these personality differences can be hugely rewarding. Yet, they are not always easy to handle.

Have you thought of the fact that 75 per cent of the people we meet in our lifetime are going to be completely different from us? However, when faced with such differences, we are surprised. We are quick to ask questions like: Why are you like that? Why can't you be more like me?

The fact is that while we enjoy differences in the short term, in the long term we start trying to change, sort or fix people to suit our own idea of how they *should* be.

There have been times in my life where I have been guilty of this too. One of those people happens to be my husband, who is also my partner at work.

Our relationship has constantly walked a tightrope between work demands and personal needs, trying to maintain the precarious balance between the two.

When he wanted to drive new challenges at work, I needed us to slow down and spend more quality time together. When he wanted to play a hippie and travel the world to enrich his life, I needed the security of work and home. While he thrived on new experiences, I craved the familiar. My need for stability provided the contrast to his ambition.

I have always known that my husband and I were meant to be different people and we consciously celebrated our individual personalities. However, at a subconscious level I had a long list of how he 'should' be as a partner. Every time my expectations were met, I loved our relationship and patted my back for the right choice I had made. However, when my list of 'shoulds' were not met, it led to anger, irritation and resentment.

Those were the times when I would try to change him to

suit my needs. For a long time, I believed that I was only trying to motivate, inspire and help him to grow, till he gently pointed out that I was trying to change him and I was fooling myself into thinking otherwise.

Think about all the energy you put into trying to change other people. Is it fun? Is it working out well for you? Probably not. All you are likely doing is focusing on the things you want changed and putting a lot of negative energy and thoughts towards it. But ultimately nothing changes, am I right?

This eventually leads to loads of resentment, bitterness, lost time and unutilised opportunities. All this can be avoided with an understanding of how to adapt to different personalities.

Is it possible to make this change in perspective? The answer is yes. You can build the awareness and acquire the skills to deal with different people, even the seemingly difficult ones, without trying to change them.

This is one of the most important lessons we need to learn to make our relationships easy and meaningful.

2

Do We Really Know People?

Are people really different or do they simply pretend to be? This was the question a client of mine asked. Struggling to deal with a situation where her husband had cheated on her with her best friend, she was devastated. Sitting in my office, the blank look in her eyes betraying the immense pain she was carrying, she told me that she and her husband were always different. She was focused, hardworking, practical, disciplined and honest to a fault, while he was the charming, funny, impulsive, lazy and occasionally manipulative one. He would depend on her to handle family demands. She would be in charge of the kids, whereas he was supposed to be the provider. 'I gave up my career to look after the house. I sacrificed my dreams and financial independence. I traded my passion to be an interior designer to be a good mother and wife.' The most painful part was that she seemed to have kept her end of the bargain, whereas he had not. She believed that while she stayed home and looked after every need of the family, he was looking after only his own.

There was something else she had discovered about him which added to her sense of betrayal. Not only was he involved with the other woman, she also found him to be very sensitive and giving towards her. And he was emotionally available for her, which he had rarely been when it came to his own wife.

'Who is he? Was he just pretending to be different with me?' was a burning question she needed an answer to.

Though not with such intensity, a lot of people struggle to understand others as small issues crop up in relationships on a daily basis. We try to figure out colleagues at work, the idiosyncrasies of the boss, the quirks of family members, friends and even our own parents at times.

Let's go back to the root of it. The way people think, feel and behave can be expressed in a single word: personality. This is a broad term that describes how people habitually relate to the world and also their inner self. Personality is a composition of traits, characteristics, needs, values, beliefs, experiences, perception and a lot more that makes us uniquely US.

The study of understanding people is an old one. The purpose of this is simple. If you can understand people, you will be able to predict how they will respond to certain situations and, therefore, be able to manage them better. You will be able to understand why they behave the way they do, their needs, values and quirks. Also, you will feel more in control of the situations around you and your reaction to them. Now, isn't that valuable? It sure was, to my client.

Personality has been spoken about since ancient times. The Ayurvedic expression of personality in the form of Sattva, Rajas and Tamas gunas is popular the world over. Astrology, the ancient shastra derived from the Vedas, also speaks about personality based on the time of a person's birth. As people, we are said to belong to the four essential elements—air, fire, water and earth. It is believed that these elements represent a dominant type of energy that acts in each of us. For example, water signs are considered to be emotional, sensitive and intuitive, whereas fire signs are seemingly passionate, dynamic and temperamental. Air signs are said to be thinkers, friendly, intellectual and communicative, while earth signs are considered to be grounded, conservative, practical, loyal and realistic.

Hippocrates, a fifth-century Greek philosopher and physician, viewed personalities as four types. They are the choleric (hot-tempered), the sanguine (confident), the melancholic (moody) and the phlegmatic (slow to act). He firmly believed that mind and body are two sides of the same coin. This was an attempt to integrate body and mental functions. In fact, in the 1940s, William H. Sheldon, an American psychologist and physician, again tried to relate the body with the mind. Broadly speaking, he classified people's personalities into three categories. Endomorphic bodies—soft and round—were relaxed and sociable. Mesomorphs—strong and muscular—were energetic, outgoing and assertive. Ectomorphs—thin and fragile—were introverted, artistic and intellectuals.

Personality has been defined and explained by various theories for centuries. The classical psychoanalytical theory of Sigmund Freud, trait theory by Gordon Allport, social learning theory popularised by Canadian psychologist Albert Bandura and the humanistic view of Carl Rogers are all examples of our attempts to understand the human mind.

Every era has produced thinkers who have invented, explained and interpreted theories that have reflected their beliefs against the backdrop of a world view.

It is important for us to recognise the attempt that each of these eminent people have made to add to the science of understanding people. While we have so much awareness of our physical and material world, our understanding of the inner workings of the mind is abysmal. Most often we are clueless about our own drives, wants, expectations and triggers, let alone those of others.

There is no manual, book, course or subject at school that teaches us about people and how to develop a deeper understanding of ourselves. That seems to be the reward that one gets after living for many years on this planet, having struggled with relationships, been burnt with challenging life experiences, felt hurt or betrayed by others and then finally woken up to the wisdom of human personality. As they say, life teaches us all.

Imagine what would happen if we could shorten the learning curve. If we could have an easy system of understanding how our mind works, decoding how the universe of people around us functions and of predicting behaviours and managing reactions, our lives would become immensely easier. Now that is something worth investing in, isn't it?

3

Like Chalk and Cheese

Most of us go through life completely unaware of how our personality defines our behaviour. For the past decade, I have been spending a lot of time on planes, travelling to new countries and working with varied groups of people. I regard my time on the plane as sacred 'me time', ideal for catching up on my reading, listening to podcasts, journaling and simply slowing down my mind. With no demands, phones, technology, networking or interruptions, this is the perfect time for me to just BE. It's my zen time as I cross several time zones.

Sitting next to me is my partner at work and in life, in a hyper-productive mode. He walks into the flight with a long to-do list. Unlike me, this is the perfect time for him to get work done. He is absolutely focused as he clears up his backlog. The success of his time on the flight is defined by the amount of work he manages to accomplish.

Each time we walk off the plane, he is ready to charge into his next assignment, while I take my time to soak in the land and its people. He walks purposefully, while I have a relaxed stride as I take in the sights, sounds, smells and the environment. If you were to see us, we would appear as two completely different energies, yet strangely harmonious as we navigate through the airport.

While my husband and I have the same job of enabling people to experience deep personal transformations, we don't go about this the same way. I pride myself on creating an emotionally safe space that allows people to shed their inhibitions. I hold them gently as they explore and express their feelings. I let them set the pace of our conversations. I help them dismantle layers of limitations as they discover a new way of being. For me, the essential ingredients in any transformative process are acceptance and compassion.

My husband, on the other hand, inspires action. He holds the vision for his clients, prods them, pushes them, stirs them, confronts them and helps them reframe their life stories. He believes in forward movement. He has little tolerance for victimhood and he tells it as it is.

Both of us pursue completely different styles, ideologies, approaches and outcomes. And yet, we are extremely effective in our own ways.

We all display characteristic patterns of thinking, feeling and behaving that, over time, come to define our personality.

When we don't understand, accept or appreciate the differences between our personality and that of others, we get stuck in a perpetual war with them. We fight, blame or attempt to change or fix others, often without any success. The emotional cost of trying to change the world is huge, and often unnecessary. We start this journey by being aware of two important facts: we are all designed to be different and we cannot change anyone else to suit our needs.

Many years ago, I thought I hit the jackpot when I found a boyfriend who was very similar to me: introverted, sensitive, thoughtful and gentle. I believed that we were in perfect harmony and had few potential triggers between us.

In some ways, I did hit the jackpot, but the excitement didn't last long. A couple of months into the relationship, I learnt that having similar personalities didn't mean that we were compatible. And it definitely didn't mean we were going to work out in the long run. Fifteen months later, we separated. I realised that even when you get together with your personality twin, it doesn't mean the relationship will be a happy one.

William J. Chopik and Richard E. Lucas studied 2,578 heterosexual couples in their attempt to determine whether the similarities between the personalities of two partners had a substantial effect on the relationship's well-being.*

Turns out, the similarity factor had very little effect.

Respect, awareness, patience and understanding were more reliable predictors of happiness. Ultimately, it boils down to what you value the most in yourself and your partner, how you communicate and how you work together as a team—not necessarily how similar you are.

This is not just limited to our personal lives. At some point in our professional lives, most of us have to deal with people we just don't like or can't seem to get along with. The differences are stark and the triggers buzzing.

Some people like to work quickly, completing their tasks as soon as they are assigned, while others like the adrenaline rush of getting to the task when the deadline is looming. Some of us are naturally upbeat and optimistic, whereas others may be extremely cautious and prone to pessimism. Some colleagues feel the need to compete while others cooperate and work together.

The fact is that personality differences exist everywhere and people are bound to have varied perspectives. There is no one right way of being or behaving. The more we fight it, the harder it becomes. The more we resist it, the stickier it gets. Instead, the more we understand it, the easier it is for everyone involved. And the more we learn about the differences between people, the less they overwhelm us.

---

* William J. Chopik and Richard E. Lucas, 'Actor, Partner, and Similarity Effects of Personality on Global and Experienced Well-being', *Journal of Research in Personality*, Volume 78, 2019, pp. 249–261, https://www.sciencedirect.com/science/article/abs/pii/S0092656618301508

4

The Art of Decoding Personalities

It takes some time to learn about the personalities of the people around you. But we certainly don't need to spend a lifetime trying to find the answer to the question 'Why do they behave like that?'

Shaan is outgoing, while Mira is more reserved. She prefers socialising in small groups, preferably one-to-one. Shaan's job profile requires him to network and socialise. Mira is often hurt and uncomfortable when Shaan makes the rounds at parties, leaving her to fend for herself, sometimes for hours. And he can't understand why she won't open up and have fun.

Ayesha is practical and pays close attention to details. She keeps a careful record of how much money is spent because she is prudent and sensible. Her partner, Sam, is rather impulsive and hates to be restricted. He loves to live in the moment and experience life fully. He is prone to spending on unnecessary things: 'After all you live only once,' he says. He feels rather frustrated when Ayesha keeps a tight rein on the budget.

Neha is quick to notice people's feelings and tries to avoid arguments. Tina is blunt, direct and enjoys a good argument. Though they are siblings, they are like chalk and cheese. Neha is sensitive, approachable and nurturing. Tina, on the other hand, is ambitious, strong-minded and focused. It frustrates her when

Neha can't set clear boundaries, and say 'No' when needed. It bothers her when people take advantage of her docile sister. On the other hand, Neha feels that Tina is too blunt, not a good listener and quick to judge.

In my experience of working with hundreds of people across the world, these kinds of conflicts are an everyday occurrence. Though these differences are common, they are not always easy to handle or resolve. In fact, over time, some of them can lead to some serious and irreparable damage.

In my own family, my sister's son is a rebel. He is creative and loves to have the freedom to experiment. Recently, he was trying to do his homework with his mother in charge. She tried to structure his school projects and made a timetable for him to follow. Her methodical mind became extremely frustrated with my nephew's inability to follow the rules. The more she pushed him to get organised, the more he rebelled. She struggled to deal with his lack of attention to details and deadlines. My nephew, on the other hand, felt extremely caged and controlled by her.

The real breakthrough for them happened when we spoke about how the differences in their personalities were playing a big role in this discord—that she did not deliberately want to be a nagging mother and he did not intentionally want to irritate her.

The goal of decoding personalities is to to understand your own needs and preferences, and then recognise how different personalities function in the world around us. That's when we can find most of the answers to even seemingly complex human issues.

It's time to start a new journey of discovery. Don't worry, this process will be a fun experience! So, let's begin with a game. The goal of this game is to help you learn more about yourself and the people you interact with on a daily basis. The rules of this game are simple:

First, look at the five shapes on the next page. Then choose the shape you most relate to—the one you feel is YOU. If you find that difficult, choose the shape you were most attracted to when you looked at the page.

Once you have chosen, write the shapes in the order of preference, from the most preferred to the least preferred, in the space below. Ready?

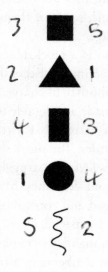

Rank the shapes

1. _____
2. _____
3. _____
4. _____
5. _____

It is important that you *write down* your order of preference, so that when you understand shape psychology later, you will be able to see how the shapes describe your personality.

5

The Woman Who Thought in Shapes

It all began in the 1970s in Tampa, USA. Dr Susan Dellinger, a dynamic, young woman, with a PhD in Communication from the University of Colorado, joined General Telephone and Electronics (GTE, now known as Verizon) as a management trainer. Brimming with enthusiasm and a desire to help the supervisors and managers of GTE communicate more effectively, she realised that she couldn't do it while sitting in her office.

She hopped on a truck with her supervisors to observe how they interacted with their cable splicers and installers on the field. Soon, it dawned on her that the real world was far different from what she had learnt in her books.

The training programmes from her university were too complicated or too conceptual to appeal to the field-bred supervisors. Also, little of what she had learnt in the classroom could be applied outside of it.

She realised that she needed to create a system that enabled people to discover personalities and identify communication styles. She wanted this new system to be simple, easy to understand and, most importantly, easy to apply. While the idea took seed, the path wasn't clear.

One day Dr Dellinger went into the classroom and drew five geometric shapes on the board. She then asked the supervisors to choose a shape that most connected with them. Next, she associated each shape with certain personality traits. It was an instant hit! The supervisors could relate to their own personality type as well as understand why differences existed.

From that day on, people couldn't get enough of this geometric psychology game. The system raced through the company. Leaders, managers and supervisors sought her out to discuss problematic employees. Suddenly, there was a new language available: the language of 'geometric shapes'.

In 1982, eight years after she walked into GTE, Dr Dellinger left the company to take her newfound magical system to a larger audience. For the next 16 years, she travelled across the globe, presenting this system to thousands of people across all walks of life.

In 1989, Dr Dellinger wrote a book on this subject called *Psycho-Geometrics*. Since then, it has been published in eight languages, including Spanish (2022).

The Psycho-Geometrics® System has been used in the US, the UK, throughout Europe, Australia, South America, Saudi Arabia, Ukraine and Russia. Multinational corporations, government agencies, universities, law firms and non-profit organisations have also been making the best of it for 30 years. And you, the reader, are now about to get introduced to it. Remember, this information can literally change your life!

Psycho-Geometrics® is based on the notion that we tend to be attracted to certain shapes based on our personality, our attitude, our education, life experiences and on the way our individual brain functions.

The next few pages will give you a quick overview of each of the five shapes and their primary attributes. On this amazing journey of self-discovery, you will have many 'aha!' moments.

The Square/Box

Welcome to the world of a square, popularly known as the Box. The most hardworking of all shapes—Boxes—know how to get the job done. They are the 'implementers'; no matter what is involved or how long it takes, once they commit to a task, they will persist till the end.

A square is composed of equal lines and angles. For this very reason, the Box tends to be the most structured of the five shapes. They are meticulous in everything they do and pay attention to detail. A Box person would probably have their kitchen absolutely organised, every bottle labelled, all the meals planned and a set predictable routine. Do you know of anyone like that?

Boxes need life to be predictable: everything in the right place at the right time.

You will find Boxes constantly trying to organise people and things around them. They truly believe in the saying, 'A messy desk equals a disorganised mind.' They hate clutter and feel flustered when things are chaotic and not in order.

A couple of months ago, my husband and I decided to buy a car. It was finally time for an upgrade to the model we had been dreaming of owning for a while. We spoke about it briefly, reviewed the colour options online and then decided on the date of purchase. That afternoon I made an excited call to my father. 'Yippie, we are buying the new car, Dad!' I exclaimed.

This was met with absolute silence on the other end. 'Dad, are you listening?' I asked.

In a steady voice, he replied, 'Yes, I am listening. This is great, but I hope you have done all your research.'

His quiet voice of reason felt like a damper to my overenthusiasm. The conversation then went something like this:

Dad: This is an important purchase. It's expensive and, after all, you have to use it for a couple of years at least.'

Me: Hmm.

Dad: Have you looked at all the different models in that price range? There are so many brands available in the market. It's best to make an informed purchase.

Me: Actually, I haven't checked the options, since we had already decided on the car we wanted.

Dad: Also, did you go to the dealer and see the possible colour options?

Me: Nope. I checked them online, Dad. They gave me six different colours!

Dad: The colour always looks very different up close. Wouldn't it be a good idea to visit a showroom and check that?

Me: Hmm.

Dad: Also, what about the payment plan? Have you done some research on that? Get some quotes from different dealers and financing options too.

Me: Gosh, Dad! This sounds like a lot of work!

Dad: Of course, it is. You can't just go and pick the first one you see. It's important to do all the research before you make a decision. If you don't have all the data, how would you know you made the right choice?

Me: (*groaning*) I like that model ...

Dad: There is no point in being impulsive. Caution is important.

Me: (*deflated*) Okayyy ...

Dad: And don't forget to file all the data and information properly. You never know when you might need it again!

By now you would have guessed that my father is a strong Box. How many of you have a Box-type person in your life? Boxes pride themselves on being extremely logical and reasonable. They are not prone to impulsive actions. Sometimes they can take a while to make a decision because they need to have all the data. They are analytical, cautious and risk-averse. They are also solid, grounded and knowledgeable.

Boxes will collect loads of information and file it under the appropriate headings so that it is properly organised. They will make decisions only after they have reviewed all the possible evidence and considered the options.

As you may have guessed, I delegated the process of buying the car to my dad. And he did a stellar job of it!

Of course, with every set of strengths, there are a few weaknesses also. The Box is better at implementing rather than creating a compelling vision for the future. A Box can execute a plan flawlessly, but is not the best at designing it.

Also, the Box can be slow at decision-making. When push comes to shove, the Box will procrastinate, particularly if the decision involves some element of risk. They will delay it till they feel they have enough data to make a sound decision. If a risk has to be taken (however small it may be), then it better be a calculated one!

Boxes do not function well in situations that are not well-defined or in a constant state of flux. The Box says, 'Tell me what the rules are, tell me what the deadlines are, give me the tools to do it and I'll get the job done for you!'

But when the situation is ambiguous, they tend to get flustered and uncomfortable. In an environment which is volatile, the Box can become rigid, inflexible and less responsive to change.

However, in situations where the instructions and requirements are clear and expectations well-defined, the Box will excel above all the other shapes.

The Triangle

The world of the Triangle is different from that of the Box. While both are linear and task-oriented, Triangles are go-getters. They are the charismatic movers and shakers in an organisation. As parents, they will push their children to excel. As spouses, Triangles need to be the person in charge and insist on getting things done their way.

The Triangle has symbolised leadership for centuries, probably since the time the Egyptians buried their pharaohs in pyramids. The pyramids are triangular, representing direct energy and power. Archaeologists also believe that the sides of the pyramids depict the rays of the sun. A triangular structure teaches us the value of focusing our energy on an important goal. This is the singular most valuable trait of the Triangle—the ability to focus on the only thing that matters.

While the Box is interested in perfecting the process, the Triangle is concerned about the end result. Also, unlike Boxes, Triangles are swift and decisive. They love to make decisions—for themselves and, if possible, for everyone else too.

Jay is a brilliant and extremely successful lawyer. He is relentless in his ambition. He has achieved more in 18 years of being a lawyer than most people do in a lifetime. He sleeps five hours a night, works six days a week, and has a low tolerance for people who seem less driven than him. When triggered, he could chew up junior associates at a record pace. While they fear him, they are also immensely inspired by him.

Probably the strongest attribute of Triangles is their ability to not get sidetracked once they set out to achieve something. While they can be true change agents in organisations and a role model for many, their aggression can sometimes hurt people.

My mother-in-law is a 'tiger mom'. Fiercely protective of her children, she has also driven them to excel. She doesn't appreciate people who cast themselves as victims. My husband shares the story of how as an eight-year-old, he came home from school complaining about two children who bullied him often. He went to his mother teary-eyed, expecting her to hug him and console him.

Instead, she listened to what he had to say and told him firmly, 'When you appear weak and scared, the world will treat you like that. The next time they make fun of you, look at them in the eye and tell them that if they ever bully you again, you will talk to the concerned authorities and make sure that strict action is taken.'

She asserted, 'You are stronger than you know. You will not allow anybody to treat you badly.'

The next day, she hauled him out of the car, went straight to the kids and waited while he told them off. She refused to buckle under any emotion till the boundaries were drawn and the kids never bothered my husband again.

If there are Triangles in your life, you are fortunate. They will ensure that you are taken care of and have nothing to fear. Your life will be a constant flow of exciting people and places. The Triangle will always strive for something better. The downside, though, is the Triangle's need for dominance and control. The fact is that Triangles can make you subservient if you are not firm and can't uphold your boundaries.

The Circle

If I had to describe a Circle in one word, it would be 'love'! Circles genuinely care about others. In a family, they are the glue that keeps people together. At work, they thrive on building mutually meaningful relationships. They do whatever it takes to make family, friends and co-workers happy. Naturally averse to conflict, they calm the waters and keep the peace. Circles also 'read' people well. In fact, they can tell if a person is not genuine within a matter of minutes!

Geometrically, the circle is the mythological symbol for harmony. And in real life, Circles hold an encompassing space for others. They have no sharp edges which might hurt others and are sensitive and caring.

My mother is a Circle. She believes that it is her job to nurture not only her children but the world at large. As a child, if I failed a test and felt really guilty about it, she would hug me and say that it didn't matter, that there were many more tests ahead that I could excel at. For her, internal feelings of comfort and harmony were much more important than external achievements.

She also has an innate sense of knowing when people are low. She instinctively knows what they need and quickly offers the right kind of support. People feel heard and understood around her. They call her when they have problems, and when they want to share happy moments too. She has been a mother figure to many, often at the cost of exhausting herself. I consider her to be the natural giver but not a graceful receiver. Does that resonate with you? Do you have a Circle in your life?

As leaders, Circles try too hard to please everyone. They attempt to keep peace and, in doing so, sometimes avoid taking the hard line and making the unpopular decision that may be necessary.

Mira, who worked in advertising for more than a decade, came to me for coaching. She was happy being a sensitive person, but it was coming in the way of her being an effective leader. 'I really have to learn to set boundaries for myself,' she admitted.

Mira worked really well in a team. She was cooperative, empathetic and patient, sometimes to a fault. She got consumed by the problems of others and went out of her way to help them. She found it hard to give honest feedback, lest it hurt someone's feelings. She couldn't bear the idea of her workmates not liking her and would spend hours worrying that she'd upset them.

The distinction between personal and professional was blurry, as everything seemed to be personal. Also, as a Circle, she felt taken advantage of by stronger, more dominant personalities like Triangles.

It was quite a journey for her to recognise that being a good leader also meant exercising tough love at times. She now makes it a point to remind herself when to step back and not get too consumed by the issues of others. She has also learnt to speak up, give authentic feedback, say 'No' when needed and balance firmness with compassion.

Well-liked by everyone, a Circle rolls through life spreading love and goodwill. The caring, empathetic, stabilising, reflective and loving presence of Circles can smoothen any ruffled feathers. Their shape is a symbol of harmony and peace. As Circles grow older, they can develop great wisdom about life and people. But that may come with its own share of pain and challenges.

The Squiggle

Now it's time to introduce the most unique of the five shapes. Squiggles are ... just different! They are the original right-brain thinkers who are unlike any of the other shapes. Not limited by linear thinking, they have the capacity to come up with out-of-the-box ideas, which makes them very creative.

In organisations they are the non-conformists, whose passion in life is to march to the beat of their own drum. They are unconventional, unorthodox, unique and unpredictable.

A few years ago, I was in a meeting with Sam, a CEO and an old client of mine. The human resource (HR) executive was updating the team on several changes to be made in the training process. 'This is going to change the way we have been approaching training in this company,' the HR executive said. Brimming with energy, she introduced some path-breaking, unconventional ideas.

As I sat in on this meeting, I noticed that two of the other managers were silent. Sam asked for their opinion on the recommended changes.

The senior manager thought for a while and then responded in a measured way, 'While I understand the need to think outside the box, it's also important to see how our processes have worked in the past. We have been getting some good results, and I would recommend that we stick to our original processes. Why change when it's not needed? Rather than introducing new programmes, we need to make the implementation of the existing training modules more robust. We need to create standard processes for everyone to follow. We should do some research on the schedules of our managers ....'

I could see the frustration on the face of the HR executive, who had been trying to drive change for a while now.

After the meeting, Sam asked me to share my thoughts. I replied, 'Your senior manager likes to stick to the tried-and-tested, whereas the HR executive is excited about introducing some new ideas. This is a classic Box–Squiggle conflict. Don't let hierarchy determine who gets their way. If thinking outside the box will provide an advantage in addressing problems, then it's worth it. Don't let the Box stifle the Squiggle's creative thinking.

Sam, who is trained in Psycho-Geometrics®, did something wonderful. He encouraged the ideas of the young HR professional (who is a Squiggle), set up some pilot groups, tested the effectiveness of the new changes and then asked the senior manager (a classic Box) to create a robust process around implementing these new changes, which were now tried-and-tested. Best of both the worlds!

In terms of daily behaviour and personality, Squiggles are

the most exciting of all the shapes. New challenges stimulate them; they thrive on variety and change. When it's a new and interesting idea, the Squiggle bounces off the walls telling everyone about it. The Squiggle is not interested in specific details such as facts and figures—that's too boring!

By the time one gets into the details, Squiggles have already jumped to what they believe is the next big thing. Squiggles also hate highly structured and regimented work environments. They are not made for routine and monotonous jobs. They require loads of variety and stimulation to do their best work.

Squiggles get bored with rules and policy manuals, and dislike being bound. They are much more interested in the concepts and vision that their work involves.

This makes it difficult for Squiggles to work in highly organised environments.

Squiggles come alive in a free-flowing, creative and independent environment. In fact, a Squiggle is an ideal employee in a start-up, where there is constant change and growth.

One of my coaching clients, a dominant Squiggle, would often forget the time of our sessions. She would keep changing the agenda, get easily distracted and find it immensely hard to follow up on what she had committed to do during the week. Keeping her on track was like rowing against the tide.

But she warmed my heart with her exuberance, her passion, her sense of humour, her easy adaptability to change and an inherent ability to look at the positive side of things.

I called her my sunshine client. That's a Squiggle for you.

The Rectangle

When I was a student of psychology, my best friend decided to get married. It was a dream come true, as she and her fiancé had been together since ... almost forever. A couple of months after the wedding, her husband got an exciting job offer overseas. They had to move out of the country to make the most of this once-in-a-lifetime opportunity.

As she packed up her life here, she told me about how overwhelmed she felt with all the rapid changes. She was finding it difficult to catch up with these huge transitions.

Three months later, she called and told me she was pregnant! Sounding excited and nervous, she said, 'It was not planned.' Her husband was still settling into his new job, and she hadn't yet decided on the course of her career.

She took the next couple of months to find an appropriate house, close the deal, move in, set up everything for the baby and manage daily chores. She felt utterly alone as she navigated through this phase. While her husband was immensely supportive, the changes within and outside of her were taking a toll.

Her baby was pre-term. She came wailing into this world 45 days ahead of time. She was severely underweight and needed intensive care. My friend would travel from home to the hospital every day, spend the day waiting on and feeding the baby and then come back home exhausted. Too tired to cook, she would gobble up some cookies with milk and fall asleep. This became her routine for the next month. Finally, the baby arrived home, but it was not easy. The little one was prone to infections.

Once things settled down (her baby is healthy and growing beautifully, she has a great job and her husband is also doing exceedingly well), she recognised this hard phase as one that propelled her growth like no other. She became stronger, wiser, patient and more independent than ever before. 'Now I can handle anything,' she says with confidence.

Over a decade of working with people, I have seen several of them go through transitory phases—some big, some small. These phases are characterised by CHANGE. Typically, you are pushed out of your comfort zone, but haven't found your new ground yet. It's like being in the birth canal. Neither are you in the warm, familiar comfort of the uterus nor have you arrived in the glaring brightness of the world. It's the dark in-between struggle that can seem unending, arduous and overwhelming. Yet, it is immensely necessary to birth a new 'you'. This is when you are in a Rectangle phase.

So, if you chose the Rectangle shape as your first choice, you probably are undergoing some major changes within yourself. You may have just experienced a career change or are anticipating it. It could also be an upheaval in your personal life. The Rectangle symbolises change and a person in a state of transition. While the other four shapes are relatively constant predictors of human behaviour, the Rectangle typifies someone who is in an 'unfrozen state'. This is someone who is dissatisfied with the way life is at the moment and is searching for a better situation.

I call the Rectangle a confused person, but this is not meant in a derogatory manner. A Rectangle is not less capable than the others; they are merely unsure of themselves in that phase. They pass through this transitional period, but it usually is a rocky road for a while.

There is a geometric reason for all of this, of course. The rectangle is not a 'pure' shape. It is an outgrowth and adaptation of a pure shape—the square. Psychologically, the Rectangle is a person growing out of the Box. Rectangles are often people who have been boxed in their jobs or lives for years, and they have become bored or resentful. They have been hard workers for a long time, and they don't feel they have received the appropriate recognition for it.

So, plainly stated, Rectangles are 'sick of it'. They are tired of doing all the work and getting little or none of the credit. Their only reward seems to be more work. This situation can apply as much to homemakers as to corporate managers.

Rectangles are people in a period of change. They are not

quite sure where this change will take them, but they are dissatisfied with their current situation and are willing to try anything they haven't before.

One striking characteristic of Rectangles is their unpredictability. If you are a Rectangle, you may experience changes on a daily basis. In fact, you may appear to others as a different person from day to day—or even within the same day! This might make it difficult for them to understand you. They may get confused by the mercurial changes in your behaviour and not know how to support you.

The good news is that the Rectangle is just a phase. Thus, it will pass. There are some very pleasant effects of this period. Rectangles experience a lot of growth that takes them to a new level. As they seek, search, learn and grow, they open up to new ideas, people and ways of thinking.

Now let's go back to the game you played earlier of ranking the shapes in the order of your preference.

Take a moment to see if you can relate to the characteristics of the shape you have chosen as your first preference. Eighty-five per cent of people are able to connect with it. Isn't that amazing? Sometimes people finish reading about their dominant shape and decide that this is not descriptive of who they are. And that's okay too.

This could happen for two reasons.

❖ You may have chosen a shape that is not dominant for you today, but it is the type of person you may be in the process of becoming. So, you may have inadvertently chosen the shape you *want to be*, rather than the one you are now.

❖ Or, you probably chose a dominant shape based on what may have recently happened in your life. It may have required you to be something you are typically not, which could have impacted your choice of shapes.

If this is true, it is a good idea to *now* choose the shapes that best describe you and rank them again in the order of preference, from the most preferred to the least preferred.

Rank the shapes

1. _____
2. _____
3. _____
4. _____
5. _____

To dive deeper into the world of shapes, let's continue on our journey of discovery. Are you game?

COMMON TRAITS OF SHAPES

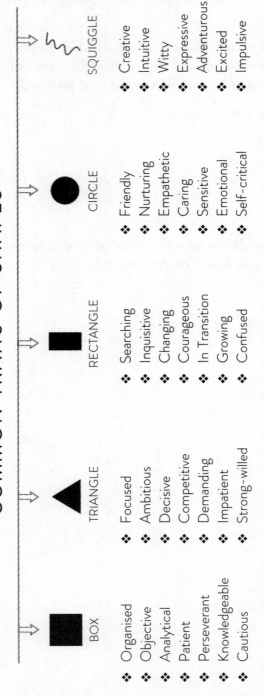

BOX

- ❖ Organised
- ❖ Objective
- ❖ Analytical
- ❖ Patient
- ❖ Perseverant
- ❖ Knowledgeable
- ❖ Cautious

TRIANGLE

- ❖ Focused
- ❖ Ambitious
- ❖ Decisive
- ❖ Competitive
- ❖ Demanding
- ❖ Impatient
- ❖ Strong-willed

RECTANGLE

- ❖ Searching
- ❖ Inquisitive
- ❖ Changing
- ❖ Courageous
- ❖ In Transition
- ❖ Growing
- ❖ Confused

CIRCLE

- ❖ Friendly
- ❖ Nurturing
- ❖ Empathetic
- ❖ Caring
- ❖ Sensitive
- ❖ Emotional
- ❖ Self-critical

SQUIGGLE

- ❖ Creative
- ❖ Intuitive
- ❖ Witty
- ❖ Expressive
- ❖ Adventurous
- ❖ Excited
- ❖ Impulsive

6

Who Are You Beneath the Surface?

Have you ever thought of people as icebergs? While you may find this metaphor amusing, trust me it's quite a deep one. Firstly, let's clarify what an iceberg is.

Many of you might know about the most iconic ship of our time, the Titanic. It is said that the Titanic received six warnings about sea ice in its path. Since the ship was travelling at about 22 knots (40 kmph), when the guards sighted the iceberg, there wasn't enough time to turn away quickly. Within a short time, a large block of ice, masquerading as a benign tip, sank the largest ocean liner of its time. This resulted in the deaths of more than 1,500 people, making it one of the deadliest marine disasters in history. All due to an iceberg!

An iceberg is a large mass of ice only a small piece of which is visible above water. In fact, on an average, only 1/10th of an iceberg is above the surface. So, if you take an iceberg at face value, it can be quite dangerous. Since icebergs float, they also tend to flip over at times. And when they do, the energy is so great that it can cause tsunamis and, on occasion, trigger earthquakes.

But does this have anything to do with people? In more ways than you can imagine. Firstly, just like the iceberg, people have a lot more going on within them than what we see on the surface. We tend to react to the obvious behaviour, moods and expressions of people. We rarely stop to think about the huge mass of past experiences, unmet needs, values, beliefs, hurt, pain and disappointments that the same people carry within them. In fact, on an average, we know only 1/10th of what makes people who they actually are.

Secondly, when we don't make an attempt to see beneath the surface, the conflicts that arise out of this ignorance can be deadly. Often it can sink relationships, families, friendships, careers and a lot more.

And thirdly, there are times when people can't take it any more. They might withdraw, get aggressive or manipulative, make rash decisions or turn vengeful. And when this happens, often without warning, the impact of it can cause huge damage to family and social systems. Often irreversibly.

Everything boils down to this: we may believe that we know our significant other, our child, our sibling or our colleague, but do we really?

As human beings, we have the innate need to categorise, classify and label people so that we can make better sense of them. Otherwise, they can seem too scary and unpredictable. Once we 'sort' them out in our mind, we believe we can understand and predict their behaviour, and learn how to manage them.

While this mental process is necessary for survival, it is also immensely limiting. Because then we start to filter out information that doesn't align with our perception of who the person is. We listen and understand selectively. We trim down that person to our image of him or her. This helps us make sense of or control our experiences with that person. This is especially true in the case of people we find very hard to comprehend.

What I'm saying is that we see only a very superficial portion of the people we encounter in our lives—be it those we are most intimate with or those with whom we share only the most fleeting of interactions.

The important question is, are we willing to look beneath the surface to explore the vast intricacies of what dwells beyond the scope of our standard view? Are we ready to let go of our preconceived view of a person to discover something totally new?

I can tell you with certainty that I am much more complex than I appear to most people. And for most of us, that complexity lies far beneath the surface, just like an iceberg.

'The tip of an iceberg looks different on a sunny day than it does on a cloudy one; it also probably looks different in the wintertime than it does in the summertime. And over time, its appearance evolves as it is shaped by the elements and environmental factors.' This beautiful description by Peter Warski encapsulates everything I believe about our hidden selves.

Similarly, I am different in different places. I thrive in sensitive, appreciative, nourishing and conflict-free environments. And I shrink in situations where strong opinions and aggressive emotions are being tossed around.

There are days when I am happy to be an extroverted person, whereas other times I am deeply withdrawn into my shell.

While I love being nurtured, I also cherish my freedom deeply. I understand the importance of change, but I also seek a lot of comfort in predictability. I am ambitious, and I also love to live a life free of any agenda.

Underneath all that people know about me, there is a part that others don't see.

The biggest strength of an emotionally intelligent person lies in the awareness that people are a *lot more* than what meets the eye. They approach each person with a sense of curiosity and compassion. They ask the question: Why do people behave the way they do? They are interested in discovering their needs, values and beliefs. And they are also curious about their own reactions to the icebergs of people.

Remember that when two people communicate, it is a dynamic experience of one iceberg connecting with another iceberg.

In the next section, let's explore the iceberg of each shape, and discover why each shape behaves the way it does.

7

The Reason Boxes Do What They Do

Let's dive deeper to understand the psychological 'iceberg' of a Box.

A Box operates from a particular kind of belief: *I need to live in a predictable world to feel in control. I want everything in the right place at the right time with no surprises.*

While as humans all of us need a certain degree of predictability, Boxes thrive on the familiar—be it a routine, a process, familiar food, known friends, favourite lounge chair or a preferred holiday destination. They are at their best when they know what to expect. This also makes them resistant to change and they are often the slowest to respond to it. Their mantra is: If it has worked so far, why change?

These type of people can be immensely challenging for those who thrive on new experiences. My Squiggle client is a bustling ball of energy. She thrives on excitement, adventure and change. Quick to get bored, she is constantly on the lookout for the next new thing. She is like a butterfly—beautiful, vibrant, vivacious and always on the move. Her husband, on the other hand, is the most stable Box I have ever seen. To me, he is like a mountain—unwavering and dependable.

On his fortieth birthday, my client decided to give him a surprise (if she had known about the iceberg of a Box, she would have never attempted this!).

She spent a month planning the perfect party. She got in touch with her husband's mates from school and college as well as his ex-colleagues. Emphasising the hush-hush nature of this surprise, she invited them to the party.

She planned the venue, his clothes, music and every other possible thing to make this a fun-filled evening. On the morning of his birthday, lounging in bed, she asked him what he would like to do on his special day. 'Nothing,' he said. 'Just lie in and enjoy some quiet time with you. In the evening, we can probably have dinner at my favourite seaside restaurant. It's so peaceful and serene there.'

This should have been an indication of what was to follow, but my Squiggle client, in her excitement, missed the cue completely. She could barely contain herself from spilling the beans of the party.

In the evening, she surprised him with new clothes (first in the line of surprises) that she wanted him to wear. He took a moment to think about the gift and said, 'Oh, you did not have to buy this. I really don't need any more shirts. My wardrobe is bursting at its seams and it's practically impossible to wear so many clothes.'

Refusing to get deflated by his lacklustre remark, she insisted he wear the new shirt, and literally pulled him out of the room.

As you would have guessed, the chorus of 'surprise!' from a huge group of people, most of whom were not intimately connected with him, was hardly a happy moment. Shocked initially, he gritted his teeth and got through the evening, struggling to converse with people he hadn't met in a long time.

The evening progressed to a surprise dance with his wife. With everyone watching them, he fervently wished he could disappear. He hated public displays of affection and found it exceedingly hard to keep smiling through the 'oohs' and 'aahs' from the crowd as they cheered on. He loathed being the centre of attention.

Late at night, on their way back home, my client and her husband had an ugly fight. Her tears, as she accused him of never appreciating anything she did, were met with stony silence. The distance between them seemed unsurmountable. 'You don't understand me at all. When will you ever get that I am NOT like you?' he said angrily.

This is not the only couple who have come to me thinking that their partner simply doesn't 'get' them. In fact, understanding the iceberg means recognising that the needs and beliefs of other people may not be the same as ours. The moment we recognise this, we are able to identify, acknowledge and meet others' needs without feeling resentful, hurt or disappointed. And when psychological needs are met in a relationship, it leads to a feeling of immense well-being.

What Do Boxes Need?

1. Routines

Boxes love routines. This is one of the significant ways in which they make their world predictable and safe. They are creatures of habit, who go to bed at a specific time and wake up at a pre-determined time, every day, like clockwork. Boxes prefer their days, including their weekends, to be well planned. If you are a Box, it is likely that you do not like interruptions, unexpected callers or last-minute changes, unless you have had a chance to plan for them.

Boxes are easily overwhelmed by the world around them. To combat the external chaos, they strive to make their world as predictable as possible.

2. Have everything in writing

Boxes like tangible things. To them, thoughts are too evasive when expressed orally. They need to see it in writing to believe it. This is also because it reflects an organised mind. So, if you want to present something to a Box, make sure you write it down. Oh, and remember to check for spelling errors and keep your margins straight. This attention to detail is one of the hallmarks of the Box personality. To-do lists are a Box's favourite. If it's recorded, it's real.

My father too has a list for everything. From professional tasks, meetings, events, outline of a conversation with his doctor, issues with the car or for the chores around the house—his varied lists keep him going through the day.

Another Box friend of mine walks around with his organiser, even on holidays! These lists help to temper a Box's anxiety about getting things done and reduce the chaos while also giving them a structure and a plan to stick to. Also, once these lists are made, it's important for a Box to display them in a specific place. Remember, Boxes have a 'correct' place for everything.

3. Planning

Boxes don't do anything without planning. If you have a Box in your life, do you remember your last vacation? I'll bet it was all lined up months ahead—the hotels, rental cars, tours, meals, etc. And paid for too! In fact, the Box makes three copies of the itinerary and gives them to important people, accounting for unforeseen circumstances. At home, Boxes like to plan household budgets and stick to them. You can never get Boxes to spend impulsively.

At work, too, Boxes like to plan things. They mitigate risk by ensuring they have covered all angles before making a decision.

They like to prepare for their meetings and have all their data available before they start. They detest discussions that have no agenda. Brainstorming exhausts them; they would prefer having things in writing, and then given a chance to think about it quietly. Boxes love flowcharts. In fact, given half a chance, they would make a flowchart for the restroom and coffee breaks.

Here is some golden advice for all those who work with a Box boss. The next time you have to tell your Box boss that your team didn't achieve its numbers, this is how you should do it:

- ❖ Describe the problem in detail.
- ❖ Gather all data and evidence.
- ❖ Put it in writing.
- ❖ Read it over 100 times to ensure there are no mistakes.
- ❖ Send it in advance to your boss for a review.
- ❖ Schedule a time for the meeting.
- ❖ Reach on time.
- ❖ Begin from the start, one step at a time.
- ❖ Be specific and logical.
- ❖ Explain how you've already tried to solve the problem and what you've learnt from those attempts.
- ❖ Clearly define possible solutions, addressing the pros and cons of each, and any potential risks or barriers.
- ❖ Explain the logic behind what you are suggesting.
- ❖ Give your boss time to think it over.
- ❖ If this doesn't work, start from step 1 again!

4. Neatness

'Who put my socks in the left-hand drawer?' If you are a Box, the one thing that infuriates you the most is when someone forgets to put one of your belongings in its correct place.

I once had a client who came in highly stressed and irritable.

She was fuming as she said, 'I can't deal with her any more! My mother-in-law is an impossible control freak!'

What started as a happy vacation with the grandchildren had clearly become a nightmare. 'What happened?' I gently asked her. 'She constantly talks of the value of being self-disciplined and having a routine. I feel like I am being judged for not having one. But I like to do what I want, when I want! She also makes subtle comments that the house is messy and disorganised. In fact, she has reorganised the entire kitchen, labelling every jar. She has made a meal plan for the week! I don't even plan the next meal, for heaven's sake!' she replied.

My client is a dominant Squiggle, and anything that is remotely Box-like makes her feel uncomfortable. Having a strong Box for a mother-in-law was driving her up the wall. But for her mother-in-law, offering to organise and help set things in order was an act of care. Interesting, isn't it?

For a Box, the paring knife always goes on the left side of the silverware drawer, the scissors are kept on the third shelf and the Scotch tape and toilet paper are always to be refilled by the person who uses the last of them. These are the rules and everybody needs to abide by them.

If you are a Box's roommate and you have a tendency to leave your things lying around, you're in big trouble! Cleanliness is extremely important to the Box. So, you better be personally clean and orderly with your belongings. Boxes cannot tolerate clothes strewn about. Do not keep your coffee mug on the table without a coaster under it.

5. Punctuality

You better be on time with a Box. This is non-negotiable. Boxes keep calendars in front of them wherever they are, fearful that they'll be late and horrified that they'll miss a commitment altogether. What annoys the Box the most are people who say 'I am on my way' when in reality they are on their way out of the shower.

My sister is chronically late for everything; I call her a 'magical thinker'. If once, during the unprecedented time of the COVID-19 lockdown, she made it to my house in 15 minutes, she now believes that's how long it should take. She promptly forgets about all the other times the journey took more than 30 minutes. That's never the case with Boxes. Being late stresses them out, and they don't like feeling out of control. They plan their schedule and are organised and systematic in a way that allows them to be on time. For a 9:00 a.m. meeting, for example, a Box will try to arrive by 8:45 a.m. or 8:50 a.m., allowing enough time for an unexpected delay, such as traffic or a full parking garage. A Box will also review directions online and check for the possibility of traffic before leaving.

Also, Boxes are unlikely to get distracted, which makes them better at time management.

6. Precision

Boxes do everything with as much precision as circumstances allow them. The carrots are cut as close to one-quarter of an inch as possible. The report is written as perfectly as possible. The night at the movies is planned with every contingency in mind (slow service at the restaurant, a line at the ticket counter, a queue for the popcorn, etc.). Work projects receive the same attention to detail. Boxes always proofread their work several times over. They like to finish their emails, memos, notes or reports in advance, so that they can give themselves time to read them multiple times over and make changes. To the Box, it's better to be safe than sorry.

They also tend to remember random details that nobody else

does. I was at a family gathering talking to some of my uncles once, and my father started reminiscing about something they did as kids, down to the minutest detail (what time of day it was and some of the things they did; mind you, this was when he was around seven years old). None of the others knew or remembered what he was talking about!

One advantage of being so attentive to details is an uncanny ability to read people's intentions. Boxes watch the people around them closely, and tend to put together the pieces of the puzzle. They rarely make their assessments based on appearances; they base their inferences on minute observations.

7. Socially selective

Boxes prefer intimate family activities, ideally one-on-one communication, to large parties. When in social settings, they drink in moderation and are often viewed by others as wallflowers or introverts. It's quite easy to spot a Box in large groups, as they are the quiet ones who can usually be found just listening and observing. Boxes rarely initiate social conversation and speak only when they feel they can contribute something of real value.

They are not party-goers and don't get a 'high' from socialising (like Squiggles). Boxes also tend to be calmer and more reserved when socialising. They speak softly, slowly and choose their words carefully, not sharing a lot about themselves. They're less emotionally reactive because they prefer to keep many of their opinions and feelings to themselves.

Common Phrases for a BOX

■

We have to do it that (right) way!

Why didn't you handle it the way I told you to?

I need to get this organised.

You need to follow the rules.

Better safe than sorry.

Meet the deadline.

If you want a job done right, you've got to do it yourself!

Save first, spend later.

Be responsible and honour your commitments.

8

If I Want Your Opinion,
I'll Give You Mine!

Now that you have a better sense of the Box, let's explore the iceberg of a Triangle.

Triangles operate from this belief: *God helps those who help themselves. So do it now!*

They don't entertain people who portray themselves as victims and believe that everything can be fixed if people put their minds to it.

My husband is a dominant Triangle. That makes him absolutely intolerant to complaints, excuses, incompetence and inaction. This is something he tells our team often: Don't come to me only with problems. Come to me with solutions for those problems.

As a Circle, I have deep respect for his Triangle energy. That is what makes him the action-oriented, go-getter CEO of our business. At a personal level though, our needs tend to clash, especially when the Circle in me feels overworked, overwhelmed or hurt.

One day I came home after taking care of my mother who had been ill. I was exhausted because as usual I had expended all my physical and emotional energy.

When I came home that evening, I had a strong urge to vent my frustration. The Circle in me just needed to be held and heard. I wanted my husband to be my sounding board, acknowledging my feelings and telling me that he understood. I'd have appreciated it if he had made me a cup of coffee and allowed me to off-load.

As I started to speak, my Triangle husband instantly started to fix the situation. He gave me solutions on how I could ensure my energy was conserved if such a situation were to arise again. I could sense my irritation growing as he animatedly tried to resolve my feelings. When I couldn't take it any more, I burst into tears and he was shocked into silence. Through the tears and all the sniffling, I told him that I just needed to be heard.

He held me close and said, 'I am sorry but I feel really helpless when you are upset. I feel compelled to make things okay for you. In my mind, I am saying that there has to be a solution to this, and I try to fix it. Vulnerability without action makes me feel extremely uncomfortable. I don't know how to help.' In those words, I sensed care, concern and also his Triangle in action.

As a spouse to a Triangle, I am always well provided for. I love his grand vision of our life together. My life is a constant flow of travel, exciting events and adventure. Nothing stays the same, as he is always striving for something bigger and better for the both of us.

'Just a cut above the rest' is the theme of the Triangle. This shape symbolises leadership, and many Triangles feel a sense of destiny within themselves: they are 'fated' to succeed! Although this life script is invigorating, the downside of this attitude is often an ambitious self-centredness that can run roughshod over anyone who gets in the Triangle's way.

True Triangles have a life history of radically changing everything and everyone they come in contact with. Both personally and professionally, they are swift decision-makers, competitive, ambitious, athletic and never happy with the status quo.

The secret weapon of Triangles is the ability to focus their energy on the goal. Even more astounding is how they are able to shift focus quickly from goal to goal. This is a result of a quick mind that is primarily logical and left-brained. Triangles become frustrated when others can't keep up with them, and many cannot, especially the Circles and the Boxes.

Triangles are not strong team players. They want to be leaders. When they are in leadership positions (assuming they are qualified for them), Triangles are capable of making massive contributions to the organisation fortunate enough to have them. While they can be true change agents in an organisation, they may not necessarily be open to feedback.

Triangles do not like to be wrong and have trouble admitting it if they are. They don't usually reverse their decisions and often fail to involve others in decision-making. Triangles constantly think about the bottom line and are quick to get to the point. They have a lot of difficulty dealing with people who waver on decisions.

Probably the strongest attribute of the Triangle is the ability to not get sidetracked. They are driven, strong personalities who set goals and achieve them. All they want is for you to get out of their way.

What Do Triangles Need?

1. To do things their way

We often refer to the Triangle as the 'executive type'. This is a person who needs to be in charge. Triangles tend to call the shots and lead from the front.

It is important to mention that not all Triangles seek dominance in the home environment. Some fulfil their need for control at work, and become truly passive at home. Both situations can be uncomfortable for those who share space with them. On one hand, the Triangle can be quite dominating, but on the other hand, they also look for peace and quiet, and expect the home to be a worry-free zone. This person cannot tolerate any problems after coming home, and the spouse better have dinner ready with a pleasant smile on their face when the battle-worn Triangle walks through the door. Either way, the Triangle is in control.

I can sum up Triangles easily: there are people who *watch* things happen, there are people who *wonder* what happened and then there are Triangles who *make* things happen!

2. Need to be right

Triangles are not the best listeners. They are impatient, especially with information or views that don't match their own. They tend to interrupt, control and dominate conversations. If you are in direct disagreement with a Triangle, you may be met with strong resistance. Triangles tend to be unbending in their views. They have a great need to be right and have difficulty admitting that they could have been wrong.

The good news is that you will always know where Triangles stand because they will not avoid conflict, which Boxes often do. An argument will surface quickly and be resolved just as swiftly. The only problem is that the Triangle usually wins.

The need to be right and be in control also makes Triangles very competitive. Anybody who is not with them is perceived as being against them, and the battle has to be won by the Triangle, of course.

While Triangles are the movers and shakers in this world,

it can come at a significant personal cost. Due to their strong need to be right, they may alienate people and inflict a lot of pain along the way. Many Triangles find themselves alone and unhappy in their sunset years. Here is an example:

Steve Jobs's brilliance, drive and passion were the source of countless innovations that enriched and improved all of our lives. He founded Apple and NeXT and took a majority ownership stake in Pixar for USD 10 million. After ten blockbuster films, he sold the company to Disney for over USD 7 billion. Around the time of his death, Apple had a market value greater than the gross domestic product of Poland! Jobs was one of the most successful businesspersons of modern times.

As a leader, Jobs was always heavily criticised for being headstrong. He was known to have a mercurial personality and was prone to emotional outbursts, typical of a Triangle. It's said that he openly showed displeasure when things did not go his way, and used silence as a way of intimidating others. He needed recognition and credit for the work he did. Some have also described him as a tyrant who was obsessively controlling. He regularly threw tantrums and openly yelled at employees and board members. It was said that his confidence seemed to be bordering on arrogance.

Yet he was also extremely bright and a passionate and charismatic leader who successfully led a company that people aspired to be a part of.

In his commencement speech delivered at Stanford University on 12 June 2005 (one year after being diagnosed with pancreatic cancer), he said, 'Your time is limited, so don't waste it living someone else's life. Don't be trapped by dogma—which is living with the results of other people's thinking. Don't let the noise of others' opinions drown out your own inner voice. And, most importantly, have the courage to follow your heart and intuition. They somehow already know what you truly want to become. Everything else is secondary.' His Triangle energy shone through!

3. Work hard, play hard

This is the motto of Triangles, who can be superb hosts and entertain lavishly at home. They can drink you under the table and yet be alert at the 7:00 a.m. meeting the next day. Don't try to play unless you can keep up with a Triangle!

Triangles can be cut-throat and demanding taskmasters, when goals have to be reached. But once results are accomplished, they can party with the same amount of energy.

Their office is full of status symbols because only the best is acceptable to upwardly striving Triangles. They want to own the latest and most expensive electronic gadgets. Triangles may never figure out how to use them, but they want them displayed prominently in their homes.

Homes of Triangles are large spaces with modern décor. They opt for top-of-the-line designers, be it for their homes or their clothes. They like to travel first-class and stay in hotels that reflect their influence and class. The lifestyle of Triangles must reflect their power, position and achievements. They love to associate with famous people who court success the way they do.

4. High energy and a fast-paced life

We all need a certain amount of stress in our lives to function effectively. In fact, if we don't have enough challenging things that excite us, we can get bored and listless. However, too much and we start to get tensed and overwhelmed. That's when we know that we have crossed our threshold. For Triangles, their appetite for challenges is far greater than that of others. They seek constant activity, and in psychological studies they are typically described as 'Type A' personalities.

Triangles cannot lie down and do nothing. For them, every minute needs to be productive. Even on vacation, they are not the kind to lay on a beach all afternoon doing nothing. They need to explore, network or go on short trips to make the most of a vacation.

Triangles need to be physically active. If they are too busy to be a part of competitive sports, they will develop a personal exercise schedule. They will push their limits and actively strive to better themselves.

Because Triangles live in the fast lane, they are prone to addictions and often tend to smoke or drink too much. They are the most prone to becoming workaholics.

Triangles Feel Most Comfortable When

- ❖ They are in control of a situation.
- ❖ They have the authority/leadership in a group.
- ❖ They are in a position to write the rules.
- ❖ Their opinion is sought by important people.
- ❖ Their work is recognised and appreciated.
- ❖ They are members of a prestigious group.
- ❖ They get to challenge the status quo.
- ❖ They are looked up to and respected.

Common Phrases for a TRIANGLE

▲

Get to the point!

What's in it for me?

You're fired!

It's my way or the wrong way.

Do as I say.

Let's get to the bottom-line.

Why are you getting sentimental?

9

Am I Too Sensitive for This World?

While the Triangle is an ambitious go-getter, the Circle is its shadow side. Let's dive deeper to understand the iceberg of a Circle.

Circles believe in the adage: *Do unto others as you would have them do unto you.* In other words, they desire a world where people accept, acknowledge and appreciate each other and where there is love, harmony and sensitivity to needs and feelings.

I have always been loving and openly affectionate. What matters the most to me, more than achievements, accolades, fame or fortune, is the love I create around me. However, wearing my heart on my sleeve has not always been easy. As a child, I was extremely sensitive to people's moods and energy. I could instantly spot when a conflict was brewing or when someone was about to get angry. I could feel the tightness in my belly as I rushed to smoothen the situation and douse the fire. I was also good at noticing a lot of minor details about people, their mannerisms and moods. This made me compassionate and overtly sensitive. Not everyone saw this sensitivity as a gift, and I would often get labelled as 'highly emotional'.

As I started to learn more about my dominant Circle orientation, my life transformed. I became keenly aware of who I was and what my 'type' was. It was then that I started to make some changes that were necessary for my growth. Here is a case in point.

Being a dominant Circle, I would go out of my way to 'circle' my husband, his family, my family, our friends, my colleagues and our house help. This would leave me completely exhausted mentally.

One night, as I sat nursing a bad headache, my husband looked at me and said, 'Do you realise how much you expend yourself on others, and the toll it is taking on your body? I would like you to know that it's absolutely okay to draw some boundaries and to prioritise yourself. People will still love you as much, if not more. And if some people have an issue with that, maybe it's time for you to evaluate whether you would like to have them on such priority in your life.'

His gently spoken words made me realise how I never had energy left for things that truly mattered to me. I was constantly responding to the needs and feelings of others at the cost of my own.

As my awareness grew, it empowered me to learn the skills and do the inner work to amplify the beautiful qualities inherent in my shape. I began to see that being a Circle allowed me to have incredibly rich relationships, and it didn't need to be at the cost of my own self.

Over time, I learnt to regulate my emotions while keeping the compassion intact. I also learnt how to protect myself from being overwhelmed by emotions and other people's energies. Being loving did not mean that I had to absorb the pain, hurt or negative emotions of people around me. I also learnt to draw boundaries and not feel guilty about it. And I continue to be a work in progress.

The fact is that Circles are the friendliest of all the five shapes. This is because they are genuinely interested in others. They are the best communicators because they are the best listeners. They 'read' people well, and they quickly establish empathy for them. A Circle will actually feel your pain with you, and will nurse you back to wellness if possible. It's very easy to spot the Circles in your life. They are warm and approachable. They smile easily, make full eye contact and nod during conversations to show that they understand you. Circles are also 'touchy-feely' people. They express their love, concern, understanding and empathy through touch. They also give the warmest hugs!

Although Circles are nurturing, caring, empathetic and generous with the world, they are not always kind towards themselves. When something goes wrong, Circles tend to blame themselves first—to the point of being miserable. This trait is most damaging to Circles.

Circles also have a tendency to accommodate others, especially in situations of conflict or crisis.

I was working with a client who was going through severe depression. I discovered that her excessive Circle was at the root of her problems. She had lost her husband when she was barely into her thirties, and was raising her young son as a single parent. When her father passed away, her mother moved in to live with her. It was extremely demanding for her to take care of her Box perfectionist mother, her son, the finances and issues at work. But typical of a Circle, she continued to accommodate. She tried to meet everyone's needs the best she could. When her sister had a tiff with her mother, she was the one to mediate and resolve it. When her brother had legal issues, she supported him mentally and emotionally. She found it hard to ask for help, and when she did ask, it was with a lot of guilt.

Her tipping point came when her son blamed her for never being there for him. That completely destroyed her spirit. She recognised that being a Circle, she had accommodated the needs of everyone at the cost of herself and what was important to her. She recognised that she could no longer pour from an empty cup.

What Do Circles Need?

1. Harmony

It is incredibly difficult for Circles to deal with conflict, either at work or at home. They want everyone to get along and like each other. In a conflict, it's the Circle who is most likely to give in first. While this restores peace and harmony in the short term, it can often lead to the Circle feeling taken for granted in the long run.

When Circles find themselves in direct conflict with another person, they suffer more than any of the other four shapes. It doesn't matter who is right and who is wrong. It is the conflict itself that is so unpleasant. Circles take it personally!

Circles will either accommodate or compromise to resolve the conflict and quickly return to their state of harmony. Accommodation often leads the Circle to save the relationship rather than to solve the problem. When Circles hear angry words being exchanged, they focus on the emotion rather than the issue at hand. This is where the problem begins. Circles will do anything to alleviate the anger, even if it means giving up their own needs or what they know is the right thing to do. While this restores harmony in the current moment, a Circle tends to lose their personal power and self-respect in the process.

It has been a huge achievement for me to learn how to stay centred, even when people are feeling angry around me. My sister is a Triangle and can express her displeasure and anger very openly. She does not feel guilty talking about how she feels or asserting her views strongly. In the early years, when I sensed a conflict coming, I would feel an overwhelming sense of anxiety coursing through my body. I would focus on the emotion and lose my ability to deal with the situation productively. My first impulse would be to withdraw, to avoid the conflict and wish it would go away. I found it incredibly hard to have a conversation that was collaborative and focused on both of our needs and feelings.

Once I noticed that it was the Circle in me that desired peace and harmony, I stopped judging myself and my reactions. I learnt to accept and acknowledge them. When I released the internal resistance, it opened the door for change to happen. Now I make it a point to express my needs and feelings, firmly and with compassion.

2. Connection and love

Well-liked by everyone, Circles roll through life spreading cheer and goodwill. They are loving and joyful people. As long as everyone is having fun, Circles love it.

Circles need people around them, so they have deep connections with family. They have friends who turn into family, and have no boundary between the personal and the professional. For them, everything is personal. When you visit the home of a Circle, it's extremely warm and welcoming. They will sit their guests down at the kitchen table and treat them like royalty. In fact, a Circle is the best host of the five shapes. You will always feel comfortable in a Circle's home.

Even as kids, Circles are openly affectionate and an absolute joy to their parents. At work, they are the ones who will have plants and photos of their family on the desk. As a Circle, I know more about the emotional life of my assistant than her own family does.

However, this need for love and connection also has a flip side. Circles sometimes get trapped in the need for approval and validation. They get caught in the desire to please others, and can get hurt and upset when they don't receive acceptance from others. It is extremely distressing for Circles when others become angry or displeased with them. That's when they blame themselves. In their lows, Circles can feel like victims and tend to see themselves as martyrs.

3. Attention and appreciation

While the core need of Circles is love, their deepest fear is being unloved and uncared for. Circles are everyone's dream friend. They place a high value on their relationships and tend to give a lot. They are helpful to a fault, and will readily be there for you if you need them. They'll babysit your kids, and even stay and take care of you when you're sick.

What matters to them is that they are acknowledged for what they do. Circles thrive on appreciation. They need to know that they matter. Circles get affected by criticism easily, which is why validation makes them genuinely happy. Subconsciously, Circles have a need to be needed. When they matter to someone, it makes them feel worthy and their sense of being valued gets a boost.

4. Reassurance

'It's all my fault' is a common thought for Circles. Circles can mercilessly beat themselves up if things go wrong. Although it's good that Circles are able to acknowledge and admit their wrongdoings, they have a tendency to overdo it to the point of martyrdom.

During these moments of anxiety and guilt, Circles need reassurance. They need to be told that they haven't caused any damage or that others don't think any less of them.

5. Expressing emotions

Circles are emotional people. They cry easily and wear their heart on their sleeve. They may cry while watching a movie or feel deeply touched by the small joys of life. They can really empathise with the feelings of others, both negative and positive.

Circles can't help but express their intense feelings. If they are not given the space and safety to express their emotions, they end up supressing them. They may wear a mask of normalcy to maintain harmony. However, eventually these emotions gather momentum and explode. As a simple analogy, when you put a lid on a boiling pot, the water will rise to the top and spill over. It's the same with Circles. If they push their feelings away, they will explode sooner or later, and more fiercely than before. For some Circles, it can be years, or even decades, of repressed emotions that bubble over at their boiling point.

Circles Are at Their Best When

- ❖ They receive lots of open affection.
- ❖ The environment at home and at work is peaceful and calm.
- ❖ They are at the centre of a loving, happy family.
- ❖ They receive genuine concern from close friends.
- ❖ They are appreciated and validated for their contributions.
- ❖ They are part of a great team at work.
- ❖ There is cooperation and helpfulness.
- ❖ People are honest with them. They hate to be manipulated.
- ❖ There is trust and respect.

Common Phrases for a CIRCLE

●

You can always count on me.

How can I help you?

Relationships are more important than anything else.

We're one big happy family around here!

Let's sit down and talk it over.

Home, sweet home.

It's all my fault!

10

Who Am I, Where Am I Going?

Let's now dive deeper and understand the iceberg of a Rectangle.

Rectangles often find themselves in a state of transition. This is a phase people experience when they are on the threshold of a major change. This change could be in their personal or professional life. As they cope with this internal storm, a Rectangle's equilibrium is off-balance. There is a sense of incredible excitement over each new day, and at the same time, there is a great deal of confusion. One thing that characterises a Rectangle is a sense of hope—for a better tomorrow and a better self.

The belief of a Rectangle is: *There is a pot of gold at the end of the rainbow ... I just know it. There are better things in life, if only I could discover what they are and how to get to them.*

Rectangles are constantly searching and growing. They are discovering new ways of thinking, feeling and behaving. In this journey, they are looking for answers to their internal turmoil. There are several life stages in which rectangular characteristics are prone to emerge: marriage, the birth of a child, the death of a loved one, loss, illness, change of job or city, or retirement. Each of these situations can force people to re-evaluate their lives. It can be a confusing time because it requires the person to adapt to a new set of circumstances.

The hallmark of Rectangles is that their behaviour can change from one day to the next. In fact, if you look closely, you will notice behaviours of the other four shapes within the Rectangle. They can be controlling like the Triangle, sensitive like the Circle, impulsive like the Squiggle or cautious like the Box. And their behaviour can change on a daily basis. Rectangles are also more likely to suffer from self-doubt and low self-esteem during this challenging time because they are constantly looking for ways to make their current situation better.

A close friend of mine discovered that her husband was cheating on her. She was pregnant at the time, and she was absolutely devastated. She tried to resolve things and save her marriage, especially for the child that was on its way. I remember the turmoil she went through as she navigated this difficult phase.

After her child was born, she decided to move to another country with her husband and make a fresh start. She was leaving a familiar country, the support of her family and the comfort of her family and friends, to give her relationship a chance. It was extremely unnerving for her, at every level. She was often on edge and unsure if she was making the right decision. Erratic and unpredictable, she went on a shopping spree to change her wardrobe overnight. This was an anomaly for a friend who always took decisions practically. She would be a Box one day (micromanaging everything), a Triangle the next day (making swift decisions and asserting herself), a Circle another day (needing a lot of warmth and love) or a Squiggle (being completely impulsive). Being a new mother who was about to move to a new country with a troubled relationship was enough to put her into the Rectangle mode. This phase lasted for two years, till she finally decided to step out of the marriage. Today, she is successful and well-settled, and looks back at this stage of her life as an incredibly tough but growth-filled experience.

One of the most wonderful characteristics of this transitional phase is the Rectangle's newfound tendency to be courageous as well as inquisitive. Rectangles will try things they've never done before. And they will ask questions that they lacked the courage to ask earlier. This allows them to make changes they would have never contemplated even a few months earlier. This is why the Rectangle phase is considered to be a beautiful pathway to a *new you*.

What Do Rectangles Need?

1. Patience from others

While a person may have been extremely sure and confident of themselves in the past, in the Rectangle mode they may seem incapable of making the smallest decision. Rectangles are also prone to changing their decisions. Today they might be sure that this is the thing to do. However, tomorrow they might move in a completely different direction. Also, they could make dramatic changes when least expected. This can be extremely unsettling for someone living with a Rectangle. It's important to be patient with the Rectangle, and to remind yourself frequently that this stage won't last forever.

2. Love and support

The one thing that Rectangles need the most is unconditional love and support. It's not easy to be in this phase and Rectangles often feel judged for what they are going through. Open conversations and lots of appreciation can really help the Rectangle tackle this phase and emerge out of it in the most powerful way. The last thing Rectangles need is criticism, as they already feel lost and deeply vulnerable. It is important to offer them compliments since this creates the possibility for Rectangles to return to a sense of well-being.

3. An eager ear

I have often heard Rectangles say, 'I just need to be heard.' Since they are going through such a difficult phase, they want to talk about it with someone. In fact, having a good coach or a mentor at this stage can be a turning point for Rectangles. A few close family members or good friends who can offer their complete presence and non-judgemental ear can make a huge difference to a Rectangle. It is important to listen and refrain from giving any strong advice unless the Rectangle explicitly asks for it. There are two reasons for this:

❖ Rectangles need to come up with solutions that work best for them. Often, their clarity increases as they speak their mind. Once the fog of confusion lifts, they usually see the path ahead. You just need to be a catalyst in the process.

❖ Also, if you offer advice, it absolves the Rectangle from taking responsibility. If your suggestion does not work, they might end up blaming you later.

So, it's important to listen with an open heart and just be a sounding board for Rectangles.

4. Time and space

A Rectangle's mood swings can sometimes be difficult to deal with. But they are extremely common in this phase. Transitioning from the old to the new can be a pretty chaotic internal process. It is common for a Rectangle to be forgetful, unsure and distracted.

One of my clients, who headed the learning and development

team at a multinational company, decided to quit and start her own consultancy. This was an absolutely new area for her, which required a fresh set of skills. She was used to being in charge and having a large team working with her. She also had the backing of the organisation and was used to having her way. But as a freelance consultant, she was a solopreneur and did not have a team to fall back on. She had to learn to handle all aspects of the business. It was not an easy ride for her. And as she went through the Rectangle phase of finding her identity, she had mood swings and significant moments of self-doubt.

She found herself getting triggered a lot more than before. She was a different person every day—sometimes a Box, at other times a Triangle, a Circle or a Squiggle. But today, as a successful consultant, she often says that it was a necessary part of her evolution. Rectangles need others to give them the time and space to feel their emotions and upheavals as they navigate through this phase.

5. Protection

During this period of growth, Rectangles are also more suggestible and impressionable. They tend to get swayed by people who seem to have it all together. Rectangles can hence be taken advantage of at this time. Stressed-out Rectangles can believe almost anything during this period and may make some changes in their lives that are ultimately harmful. So, it's extremely important for the people close to a Rectangle to guard them against these bad influences or from taking impulsive actions.

What Rectangles Really Need

- ❖ A stable home environment.
- ❖ Lots of compliments and positive reinforcement.

- ❖ Space to talk about their problems and insecurities.
- ❖ Celebration of their achievements, big or small.
- ❖ Suggestions and ideas to stimulate their thinking.
- ❖ Belief that they will eventually come out of this phase stronger and wiser.
- ❖ Constant support in every possible way.
- ❖ Professional psychological help, if needed.
- ❖ Humour and the willingness to keep it light.
- ❖ To feel safe in a world that will allow them to change.

Common Phrases for a RECTANGLE

I just can't decide.

Why do we do it this way?

What do you think?

Can we talk ...?

Seek and seek and seek—and maybe ye shall find.

I still haven't figured out what I want to be.

11

Those with a Wild Heart

There are times when Squiggles can be mistaken for Rectangles. Let's dive deeper to know why, and understand the iceberg of a Squiggle.

If you live with a Squiggle, there is *never* a dull moment in your life. They are usually brimming with a lot of energy and are the happiest when something new and exciting is going on. And if there is nothing, Squiggles will create it. Squiggles love change; they are spontaneous and witty, and also exhausting! Especially to a Box.

Their belief is: *The world is a complex and exciting place to live in. There is always something to learn and to become.*

Squiggles are dreamers. To them, life has no boundaries. They are futuristic in their perspective and are years ahead than the rest of us in their thinking.

My mother-in-law is probably one of the most dynamic Squiggles I have ever met. She is extremely progressive in her thinking and not bound by the limitations of the world around her. Even though she belongs to a traditional family by birth and marriage, she has never been restricted by customs or boundaries. She finds it easy to move with the times and has no qualms about embracing change. The word 'should' doesn't feature in her life.

Even when faced with disappointments, she always finds a

way to be upbeat and motivated. She is what I call a forward thinker. And even though she does get emotionally affected by past actions, failures and mistakes, her focus is always on what lies ahead.

One of her classic Squiggle traits is that she is always in a hurry. There is so much to do and so little time! She is always running, not wanting to miss a moment of any experience that comes her way.

It is very common for her to misplace her mobile phone, forget her keys or fail to remember where she kept something. She once took a U-turn to come back home and get some papers for her 9 a.m. visa appointment, only to realise that the papers were sitting at the bottom of her purse the whole time! Since they have so much going on in their mind, it's easy for Squiggles to be disorganised. They just get lost in their own ideas and thinking.

My husband often complains that his mother tends to constantly interrupt and doesn't listen to what others around her are saying. But the fact is that the Squiggle's mind is constantly on the go—to the next new idea, the next new thought, the next new action. So they find it really hard to be patient.

If there is a party, or a gathering of family or friends, my mother-in-law is always at the centre of it. Because of her natural energy and wit, she comes alive in social settings. She is an extrovert who will talk to everyone, particularly if the person is willing to hear about her new ideas and thoughts.

Squiggles like to think of themselves as different from others. And the worst thing you can do to them is call them 'average' or 'common', when they would rather be described as rebels.

One characteristic that defines my mother-in-law is her need for constant stimulation, both professionally and personally. She has an incredible urge to try out new things. She constantly seeks out new people to interact with, new projects to challenge herself with, and new activities to engage in. That is also why she gets bored easily.

She has had several careers, and excelled at all of them. As her children were growing up, she wanted them to get exposed to a lot of experiences, beyond academics. She took them for swimming lessons, enrolled them for singing classes, encouraged them to dance, signed them up for horse-riding classes, chess, table tennis, theatre, art and much more! She wanted her kids to partake in the excitement she felt about anything new. She got them to try everything, but they never mastered any of them. Do you know why? Because she got bored of it!

As her children grew older, my mother-in-law found herself getting restless. Needing fresh stimulation, she decided to become a teacher. She homeschooled several children and did a fabulous job of it. Till this day, many of them talk about her as the best teacher they had. After all, being a Squiggle, her teaching style also had to be innovative.

Just when her Box husband thought that she had settled into this new routine, she got bored and decided to switch her career. The next new challenge was to invest in stocks. She would spend the entire day analysing the markets, future trends, companies, and the stocks she invested in. High on adrenaline, she would shift from excitement to intense concentration in a matter of minutes.

Gradually, she got bored of that too, and it was time for a new experience. Squiggles firmly believe life is too short, so they need to make the most of it. The next project was to learn professional singing. She enrolled herself in three different training classes to keep the variety and excitement going. She invited friends over and had wonderful jamming sessions. She plugged her earphones in and sang throughout the day. She attended concerts and went to karaoke parties. She motivated others to sing and eventually founded her own club of home singers. True to her Squiggle self, she named this club 'Passion'. Currently, her life is full with activities and experiences, but I can sense the boredom seeping in, and soon she will be looking for the next new thing.

A core need for the Squiggle is freedom. Squiggles fear being boxed in and will try to make sure they never are. If you are living with a Squiggle, never build an expectation of how things 'should' be with them. They are unlikely to meet them. Squiggles like surprises. You may spend a lot of time preparing a lovely dinner, and your Squiggle partner might come back from work and say, 'Turn off the oven. We are going out tonight. Let's try the new place by the seaside!' You have to be very flexible when you live with a Squiggle.

Doing the same old things the same old way is very boring for a Squiggle. Squiggles never want to maintain the status quo, for change is their lifeblood.

What Squiggles Really Need

- ❖ A good amount of excitement in their lives.
- ❖ Freedom from rules and limitations.
- ❖ Constant stimulation and variety, both professionally and personally.
- ❖ To be recognised by others as intelligent and/or creative.
- ❖ To be seen as unique and different from others.
- ❖ Open and honest expression of feelings.
- ❖ Humour and lightness.
- ❖ New challenges, new jobs or activities.
- ❖ Enough time alone to think and revitalise themselves.
- ❖ To experience, explore and discover life.
- ❖ An adoring audience for their flamboyant and dramatic personality.

An important lesson here is that it is necessary to approach people as 'icebergs'. To know that they are *more* than what meets the eye and that, for deeper connections, it's worthwhile to discover what's beneath the surface. When we take the time to truly know people, the payback is immense. Just seeing the tip of the iceberg and assuming it to be the whole person doesn't give you a window into their true personality. You never get to understand people's view of the world, what hurts them, what excites them, what scares them or motivates them, if you don't look beyond the surface.

Approaching people with a sense of curiosity and wonder is a beautiful way to discover them.

Common Phrases for a SQUIGGLE

I've got a great idea!

I will do it because I feel like it.

You're not the boss of me.

Paperwork is a waste of time!

Don't say no until you hear me out!

Rules must be broken.

Freedom is my discipline.

12

All About Love

After working with hundreds of couples, studying scientific data, and theories on marriage and intimate partnerships, one thing has become clear to me—relationships can be baffling at times. Thousands of people marry every day, committing to a lifelong relationship that they hope will be full of friendship, joy and love. But it doesn't always work out that way.

Bitterness, frustration, resentment, the pain of unmet needs and boredom kill the hope and joy that couples begin their journey with. Some years later, they turn into shadows of the people they envisioned themselves to be at the beginning of their marriage.

The fact is that all human beings have a desire for healthy, happy and loving relationships. But we are never taught how to *create* them. There is a science to it. In fact, John Gottman, foremost researcher of marriages and families, can predict with 94 per cent accuracy whether a relationship will survive the test of time or not. Amongst other things, an important factor that determines the health of a relationship is the ratio of positive to negative interactions between partners.

An important question is: Why do negative interactions happen in the first place? Don't we all hope to be together with our partner and have it all work out smoothly? The answer is always 'yes'. The problem is that we hope everything will happen magically, without us having to make the effort. That is what soulmates are all about, isn't it?

No, that's not true. Soul connections are created consciously, every moment, every day. They need intention and action. They require us to understand each other as people, recognise our differences, celebrate our uniqueness, and also learn how to accept each other's personality traits and quirks, even if we may not agree with them.

As a psychologist, I have witnessed how differences can create immense friction in a relationship, and how the inability to understand and respect these differences can tear people apart.

When the chasm between two people grows, it becomes that much harder to repair the damage caused by accusations, criticisms, judgements and labels. Sometimes the bitterness grows so deep that it becomes impossible to see the person behind all the things that we dislike. Everything that the person says or does triggers us. Have you ever felt that way?

In relationships, we often end up feeling angry, confused, betrayed or hurt. This happens when we can't make ourselves heard or when we don't have the capacity to listen to the other person anymore. That is when relationships reach a crisis point.

When a couple is caught in that kind of quicksand, there are only two possibilities. Either the partners walk down the path of withdrawal and indifference, or they use this as a wake-up call and refuse to give up until they learn how to connect and communicate with each other.

A perfect relationship is an illusion. What we should aim for instead is a wholesome relationship. And that requires conscious work. The only way to experience the incredible richness of this journey is to recognise how our personalities and histories impact our relationships.

The next section is especially important for getting a peek into how each shape relates and connects in a relationship.

13

Living with a Box at Home

While each one of us has some Box-like tendencies—
organising the house, cleaning our cupboards, doing our
taxes and planning our meals—we don't do it with as much ease
as the Box. The difference between Boxes and others is that the
former is in a constant mode of organising.

If you are living with a Box, this section will be especially
important to you. Here are some typical characteristics of a Box.

A Neat Freak

Boxes need to live with people who are clean and orderly,
especially with their belongings. They simply cannot tolerate it
when clothes are strewn around and things are not kept in the
right place.

My Box father-in-law hates it when anyone else touches his
drawers. He is meticulously organised, with everything in its right
place, neatly labelled and colour-coded. On the weekends, when
he is at home, his keen Box-like eye for detail spots everything
that needs to be cleaned, repaired, replaced or reorganised.

This is a huge trigger for my mother-in-law who, as I
mentioned earlier, is a dominant Squiggle. She is not attentive
to details and is often disorganised. She finds a sense of freedom

and fluidity in chaos. Their opposing personality traits makes life stressful for both of them.

Stickler for Routine

Another thing that is important to a Box is a workable routine. They do not like surprises or unplanned changes. My Box father-in-law has been following the same predetermined routine for the last 20 years—wake up at 7 a.m., get dressed and get to breakfast at 8 a.m., reach office at 9 a.m., have lunch at 1 p.m. (no matter what), drive back home at 6 p.m., rest for a while, go for a walk at 7.30 p.m., eat dinner at 9 p.m. and get to bed at 11 p.m. This routine gives him a sense of control and balance, and is a very important stabiliser of his life.

He expects (rather, hopes) that every member of the family will also follow a routine, and finds it hard to understand that the rest of us don't share the same need. My Triangle husband, who marches to the beat of his own drum, usually ends up defying this expectation, much to the annoyance of his father.

Keep within Means

For a Box, it is extremely important to plan and stick to household budgets. A Box needs to know whose money goes for what, and why. Since Boxes are highly practical people, it is unlikely that they will be willing to spend hard-earned money on frivolous things. This can be frustrating for other shapes (Squiggles who are given to impulsive spending, Circles who are prone to emotional spending and Triangles who are prone to flamboyance). It must be said though, that Boxes respect traditional holidays and will not deny you pleasure on special occasions.

Boxes follow the motto: Do not save what is left after

spending; instead, spend what is left after saving. Boxes are concerned about security. Box partners will always plan for retirement. They will make very calculated personal investments, and fixed deposits are a preferred choice. In addition, Boxes will be able to tell you, down to the penny, what their investments are worth.

While this approach serves them well in the long run, it can get extremely frustrating for a partner who may not subscribe to this ideology. My Squiggle mother-in-law loves the idea of spending now, in the belief that the future will take care of itself. For her, it's important to seize the moment and make the most of it. She finds her Box husband's need for moderation and control extremely limiting. She often complains quite bitterly about his inability to have an 'abundance mindset' towards spontaneous spending.

Prefer the Tried-and-Tested

True to a Squiggle, my mother-in-law loves to travel and is always ready for an adventure. She thoroughly enjoys exploring new places. The idea of new people, new lands, new food, new sites and new opportunities for experimenting is marvellous to a Squiggle. For a Box, though, the ideal vacation is at home. Boxes are not interested in cruising to exotic places, and certainly not in spending impulsively on impractical vacations. Of course, Boxes are happy to make the required trip to meet the relatives during vacation week (ideally, the same time every year) because they see it as a part of their duty. Other than that, they prefer to stick with the tried-and-tested.

Boxes are not risk-takers, and this applies to food too. No fusion food or flaming apricots for them! My father-in-law prefers to eat at his favourite restaurant (which has been his 'preferred' since eternity!) and would rather order the same dish than experiment.

Social Exhaustion

Boxes find social events exhausting, unless they involve a small circle of people. They choose their friends carefully. Boxes like to stick close to home and enjoy having a few friends or family over. My Squiggle mother-in-law has a huge circle of friends, whereas my father-in-law will go with her only if he is forced to, and grudgingly, after a lot of cajoling or tearful persuasion. Even then, she needs to be prepared to carry the ball while socialising. My father-in-law prefers to leave early, unless, of course, he has found another Box to chat with.

If the party is necessary, be sure it is planned weeks ahead. Don't expect your Box partner to be the life of the party, but do expect a thorough analysis of the way the party was organised, on the way home! Also, remember to *never* overindulge. A drunken spouse at a formal party is a Box's nightmare.

Controlled Display of Emotions

Boxes do not like to display affection in public. In fact, they prefer to avoid emotional displays of all sorts. The Box considers emotions to be private and finds all sorts of PDA offensive. As a dominant Circle, this is quite challenging for me. While I know that my Box father-in-law adores me, he doesn't often express it verbally. I get glimpses of it through his subtle actions of care and concern.

Practical Gifts

We all love to receive gifts, don't we? Triangles love to receive expensive gifts that reflect their status and achievement; Circles love a handmade, personalised and thoughtful gift; Squiggles love something unique and quirky, but the Box prefers to be *practical*.

Once, my father-in-law bought his wife a new microwave for their wedding anniversary!

The takeaway here is to avoid the temptation to buy a Box an expensive watch, a silk tie or a designer bag. These showy, impractical things do not appeal to a Box. They would rather receive practical and reasonable gifts, and tend to value them much more.

Strengths of Box Mates

- ❖ Calm and consistent.
- ❖ Predictable behaviour and routine (not prone to highs and lows).
- ❖ Disciplined, hardworking, a good provider.
- ❖ Committed approach to marriage and parenting.
- ❖ Conscientious and ethical.
- ❖ Always keep their word.
- ❖ Steadfast and dependable in every sense.

Allowable Limitations of Box Mates

- ❖ Rigid about the 'right way' of doing things.
- ❖ Resistance to change because old ways are the best.
- ❖ Low risk taker.
- ❖ Overprotective of family.
- ❖ Serious and occasionally melancholic.
- ❖ Possibly tight with money, and an overemphasis on security.
- ❖ Conservative and traditional in views and approaches.

How to Thrive with a Box

Here are some useful strategies for a successful relationship with a Box:

❖ Provide a basic, dependable, predictable home environment as a base to make the Box feel secure. Boxes find it uncomfortable dealing with a constantly changing or chaotic home environment.

❖ For hardworking Boxes, respect for their work and contributions is important. So make sure that your Box partner knows that they are respected by others and loved by you.

❖ Boxes are the most ethical of all the shapes. They hold on to their values strongly, so don't push them to compromise. This will result in resistance and a stronger position being taken.

❖ When problems arise, approach your Box with unemotional, logical and rational suggestions for solutions. Boxes find it difficult to deal with emotions and tend to freeze when there is an overwhelming expression of emotions. Provide objective data whenever possible. It's far better to state the specific things that you don't like about a situation rather than rant generally over how bad it is.

❖ Don't surprise your Box. Boxes are not comfortable in situations of spontaneity. Let them in on your plans and give them enough time to come to terms with it.

❖ Don't press for immediate action or quick decisions. Give Boxes time to think, evaluate and consider all aspects of the problem. Be patient with their questions and need for details.

❖ Do not argue with your Box in public. They hate to feel disrespected. Also, Boxes are extremely private and tend to be uncomfortable around others. A public showdown will be quite embarrassing. Wait for a time when you can speak to the Box in private.

❖ Do almost everything in moderation. Boxes respect self-discipline and abhor excesses. Do not drink, eat or smoke too much in front of them.

How to Bring Your Box Out of the Box

Here are some easy insights into how you can help your Box mate emerge from their box.

Remember to tread lightly because the Box does not change quickly. But with the right approach, some degree of change is possible if the Box aligns with it. The objective of this change is to help a Box evolve to their best possible self.

❖ Slowly encourage your Box to expand their ability to accept a larger circle of friends. At a party you've thrown, be sure there is at least one other friend who the Box is comfortable with. This gives your partner a measure of comfort. Once the Box has become comfortable with the idea of social gatherings, you can begin to include a few more people.

❖ Make it okay to talk about feelings. Of the five shapes, the Box is the least likely to share their feelings and the Circle is most likely to do so. If you are in a Box–Circle partnership, this may be the source of many of your problems. Boxes will avoid direct confrontation whenever possible, while Circles want to talk about what's happening to them.

To help the Box, one has to begin the conversation with hard data and logical reasoning. Don't get overly emotional or have an outburst. By creating this secure environment, the Box will learn that it's safe to receive and share emotions. Your Box will then slowly learn that it's natural to express feelings and that it is not a sign of weakness. Appreciate the Box when they make the effort, you know how tough it is.

❖ Encourage your Box to listen to other points of view. This isn't easy, particularly if the Box has made a firm decision about something or if the new view challenges some deeply held beliefs.

This can be done with patience and by presenting information as *objective data*. In order to succeed here, you must remember the fact that Boxes are highly linear and analytical. They are capable of processing new information and changing their views as long as the change is reasonable and logical. That's why it is important to present the new data unemotionally.

Watch your *timing*. It is best to approach Boxes before they have made up their mind about something. During the data-collection phase, Boxes are excellent listeners and will be most open to your perspective. However, once they have taken a position, they can be very stubborn about changing it. Lay stress on similarities in views, not on differences.

❖ Encourage them to develop a sense of humour. Boxes do have one, but it is often hidden behind their tendency to take life (and themselves) too seriously. Help your Box practise a lightness of being. Boxes can crack awesome jokes with a straight face! Create a sense of ease around Boxes, so that they can express their dry humour.

My sister-in-law is a digital marketing consultant. Highly achievement-oriented, she was having an animated conversation with a client. My Box father-in-law was sitting next to her. Once she disconnected the call, he said to her with a poker face, 'Here, listen to this ...

'One day, a shepherd was herding his flock of sheep, guarded by a sheepdog in a remote pasture, when suddenly a brand-new BMW appeared. The driver, a young man wearing a designer suit and Ray-Bans, rolled down his window and asked the shepherd,

"If I tell you exactly how many sheep you have in your flock, will you give me one?" The shepherd looked at this city man, then at his peacefully grazing flock and replied, "Sure. Why not?"

'The young man then parked his car, pulled out a MacBook, connected to the internet, surfed a NASA page and zoned in on the GPS satellite navigation to get an exact fix on his location. He then sent the information to another NASA satellite. Soon, he got an ultra-high-resolution photo of the area.

'This young man then opened the digital photo and exported it to an image processing facility in Germany. Within seconds, he received an email that the image had been processed and the data stored.

'Finally, he printed out a full-colour report on his hi-tech, miniature LaserJet printer and turned to the shepherd and said smugly, "You have exactly 559 sheep!"

'"That's right. Well, I guess you can take one of my sheep," said the shepherd.

'He watched as the city man selected one of the animals and looked on amused as the young man put the animal in the back of his car.

'Just as the young man was about to leave, the shepherd said, "Hey, if I can tell you exactly what your business is, will you give me back my sheep?" The city man thought about it for a second and said, "Okay, why not?"

'"You're a Digital Marketing Consultant," said the shepherd. The young man was flummoxed. "Wow! That's correct! But how did you guess this?" he asked.

'"No guessing required," the shepherd answered nonchalantly. "You showed up here even though nobody called you, you wanted to get paid for an answer I already knew, to a question I never asked, and you don't know crap about my business. Now please give me back my sheepdog!"'

My digital marketing consultant sister-in-law was in splits.

And my father-in-law said all this with a straight face, which made it even more amusing!

- ❖ Encourage spontaneity. Boxes prefer to stay with the familiar rather than try new things. Getting the Box to step out of the box is not easy. Start small. Plan an event that requires some degree of spontaneous behaviour, like dining at a new restaurant or a 'spur of the moment' movie or a weekend trip. Do it gently. Put the Box in a situation where small, spontaneous decisions must be made. Make sure you and others support the Box's decisions. This will help your Box partner develop confidence in their ability to be spontaneous.

As your Box grows more confident, their risk-taking degree will increase as well. Eventually, the Box will agree to calling friends at the last minute or maybe even consider changing jobs! These are scary things for Boxes to do at first, since it is outside of their normal behavioural pattern. But with some patience and compassion on your part, you can help your Box partner get out of their rigid mindset.

Overall, your Box partner is a very supportive, dependable and constant companion. It pays to remember that each shape has its own strengths and weaknesses. *It's what you choose to focus on that creates your own experience.*

Also, each shape has the capacity to evolve and transform. But the momentum of this change has to be built on a solid foundation of trust, love, acceptance and respect.

BOX: How to show me LOVE

———————————   ■   ———————————

Be patient and don't rush me.

Tell me and show me that I am valued and respected.

Don't argue with me in public.

Be on time!

Talk to me without getting overly emotional.

Don't surprise me.

Don't expect me to compromise on my basic values.

Give me time to think before making decisions.

Be clean and orderly with your personal belongings.

Don't expect me to be a social butterfly!

14

What to Expect from Your Triangle Partner

Radhika (whom I affectionately call Rads) is my investment consultant. She is also a good friend and a quintessential Triangle. She is impatient, driven and competitive. She has the courage to call a spade a spade. Confident and energetic, she is perpetually on the move. She rarely takes a moment to relax, and if she ever sits down without doing something useful, she ends up feeling guilty about the wasted time.

Sometimes, she can get so preoccupied with getting ahead that she seems demanding and uncaring to someone who doesn't know her well. However, I know that she is the one I will always reach out to if I need honest feedback or help in making sense of my life or just getting things done.

Her husband, Kevin, is also a great friend. He is the more laid-back and relaxed partner. He is gentle in his approach, a thoughtful conversationalist and an incredible cook. He is patient and calm, which makes him a great listener. Kevin is an artist who can get lost in the world of creative art for hours. He calls it his 'happy space'. He is also the warmest host I know.

Things have not always been easy between them. Rads fell in love with Kevin because he was so different from her. Afterwards, she would wonder why he couldn't be just a little more Triangle, like her.

She couldn't help feeling that he needed to be more aggressive, fast-paced, in control and action-oriented. He, on the other hand, found her boundless energy exhausting. The fact that she wouldn't listen, interrupted often, and jumped in to fix problems drove him nuts.

Many Triangles get attracted to the gentleness of Circles, who are happy to accommodate their needs. The problem occurs when long-suffering Circles, who have sacrificed their needs, start to get resentful about it. Triangles hate to be made to feel guilty and often believe that the Circle *chose* the supportive role.

Over time, Rads and Kevin recognised (with help from *Psycho*-Geometrics®) that these contradictory dispositions actually complement each other in a beautiful way, and could enable them to achieve a wholesome togetherness. The beginning of this process always lies in awareness and acceptance of our innate differences.

Strengths of Your Triangle Mate

- ❖ High energy and 'can do' attitude.
- ❖ Work hard and party harder.
- ❖ Firm commitment to others.
- ❖ Quick thinking and fast decision-making.
- ❖ Confident and self-assured.
- ❖ Practical, common-sense approach to life.
- ❖ Successful.

Allowable Limitations of Your Triangle Mate

- ❖ Inability to admit mistakes.
- ❖ Temper tantrums.
- ❖ Need to be in control at all times.
- ❖ Impulsive decisions.

❖ Refusal to show vulnerability (consider it as a weakness).
❖ Absent from family activities as work is always more
   important. Even if present, can be distracted.
❖ Not very open to feedback.

Triangles can be charismatic, and role models for many. Having
said that, Triangles can also self-destruct or destroy others in
their path if left to their own devices. Since they don't allow
themselves to become vulnerable or get emotionally close to
people, their partners have a huge role to play in their well-being.
Here are some insights into how you can soften the sharper edges
of your Triangle mate.

How to Live Happily with Your Triangle Mate

❖ Be a good listener. Triangles need to tell people what
   they think. If you are open to listening first, then your
   Triangle will be more open to *your* ideas later.
❖ Don't try to prove the Triangle wrong. Triangles don't
   admit their mistakes and hate for their competence
   to be questioned. If a Triangle gets into an argument,
   don't argue back, as the Triangle will always seek to win.
   Instead, wait for an opportune time and then suggest it
   as a point of view the Triangle may not have considered
   before.
❖ Don't talk about a problem unless you have thoroughly
   analysed and thought about it. If you don't have your
   facts straight, the Triangle will lose respect for you.
   Don't expect your Triangle mate to be sensitive while
   you rant. They will be quick to solve the issue. Also,
   present multiple perspectives and ideas to solve it.
   Sometimes, Triangles can get stuck to one way of doing
   things, so this gives them an opportunity to expand their
   perspective.

❖ Don't take everything they say personally. Sometimes, Triangles can be extremely blunt and may hurt the feelings of others without even realising it. Develop your inner strength and stop taking their directness personally. Trust me, it's *never* about you. Also, learn to take care of your needs. There are times when Triangles can be self-centred and lose sight of the needs and emotions of others around them. Assert your boundaries firmly but respectfully, as and when needed. The Triangle will make you subservient if you are not firm enough.

❖ As parents, Triangles can push their children too hard. They want them to be high achievers even when the child may not be ready for it. This can create friction and negative feelings on both sides. As a Triangle's partner, you may need to intervene to soften the situation. After all, a Triangle needs to accept that other shapes have their own needs and aspirations (especially their children), which may be different from their own.

❖ To enhance the relationship between you and your Triangle partner, work on creating a positive home environment in which both of you can thrive.

As Radhika said to me, 'When I started to see Kevin for who he is and cherish his uniqueness, I stopped nagging or trying to fight his battles for him (which he never asked me to fight anyway). I find that I can appreciate his talents and strengths much more now. In fact, I see great strength in him, in the way he displays endless patience without trying to check things off a to-do list like me.'

It's beautiful when Triangles start to feel safe enough to appreciate their life and relationships, and also when the people in their lives recognise the Triangle's immense potential. If you give your Triangle your love and support and still maintain your own self-respect and esteem, you will develop a relationship that can be gloriously fulfilling for a lifetime.

TRIANGLE: How to show me LOVE

▲

Be a good listener. I like to tell you what I think.

Don't take my anger personally.

Be clear and confident.

Don't argue or compete with me.

Let's face problems together instead of taking opposing positions.

Have high energy and be open to possibilities.

Don't play a victim!

Let's share big dreams.

Share your fondness and admiration of me.

When you present a problem, have all your facts straight.

15

Handling the Good Ol' Circle Partner

If there is a strong Circle in your home environment, you are fortunate! This is the person who truly cares about others, whose primary purpose in life is to help, nurture and serve.

The home is a Circle's province. Classic Circles are homebodies; they create a loving environment where there is a lot of warmth, tenderness and goodwill. Their home is one place where anyone can let their guard down, be vulnerable and admit mistakes.

The home of a Circle will have warm tones, plants, an earthy feel, antiques, heirlooms and overstuffed chairs and corners where one can relax and reconnect. The walls of the home are usually decorated with photos and memorabilia they have collected over time. Everything that they put up has significance, memories and an emotion attached to it.

In the home of a Circle, there will always be a continuous supply of a variety of foods. Circles are marvellous hosts and will never have their guests fall short of anything. Circles prefer home-cooked meals to gourmet restaurants. Circles also hate being limited to a tight budget. They need funds for anniversaries, birthdays, housewarmings, new babies, etc., because they are generous gift givers. Their lack of attention to detail means that the chequebook rarely balances. And they really don't care!

Circles aren't about money; they just want to have enough to attract others to them.

Circles hate becoming slaves to a hectic lifestyle. The world has become too busy and hectic for Circles. They love to relax and do nothing at all. This can drive a Triangle or a Box crazy, but the Circle is perfectly content lying on the beach all day or just lazily puttering around the house all weekend with no particular plans.

Your Circle partner will probably have few established routines. They don't set routines because they feel that they must always be open to the changing needs of others. You can call a Circle at a moment's notice and they will always try to be there for you.

Circles are ardent volunteers. If any group or non-profit association needs help, Circles will be the first to raise their hand. They would prefer to give their time rather than money. That way, they have the opportunity to contribute and be appreciated for their efforts.

Circles struggle to set boundaries. They find it hard to say no and end up sacrificing or accommodating more than what they can handle. Tara, a client of mine, once emailed me:

> I am married to a great guy and have an adorable son. But for the last couple of months, I have noticed that I feel really sad and let down. That is because I feel taken for granted. People expect me to be there for them, to be compassionate, be understanding and take care of their needs. But I don't feel that people care for my needs with equal sensitivity.
>
> I have always had trouble setting boundaries. I am so hardwired to take care of the needs of others that at times I don't even recognise my own needs, let alone insist on getting them met. For me, giving love comes easier than withholding it.

The times when I have set my boundaries, be it with family or friends, they have not taken it well. The common response I get is: 'Hey, what's wrong with you? Why are you behaving like this?' That makes me feel guilty and I start to wonder if something is wrong with me.

Because of all the giving, I feel exhausted and overwhelmed. And then I tend to take it all out on my son. I get irritable and short-tempered with him. And then that adds to the guilt! Is something wrong with me? Can you help?

As I read the email, I knew I was talking to a Circle. Tara and I did some amazing work together on discovering why Circles find it hard to set boundaries, and how to do it with love and compassion. She created a wonderful affirmation that she repeated to herself every time she felt self-critical or cornered: *'I am doing the best I can with the knowledge and awareness I have at the moment, and I am learning and growing.'* It was wonderful to see her evolve into a clear, strong and compassionate person.

Inherent Strengths of Your Circle Partner

- ❖ Loving and generous.
- ❖ Genuinely concerned. Circles will put you first!
- ❖ Loads of empathy. Circles are very sensitive to the pain of others.
- ❖ Open-hearted listening. If you want to talk, the Circle will listen.
- ❖ Loyalty and commitment.
- ❖ Circles will nurture anyone back to their emotional and physical health. They love to give and be needed.
- ❖ When there is conflict, Circles will work hard to keep the harmony.
- ❖ Circles can be very trusting. Unfortunately, this is how the more powerful shapes take advantage of them.

❖ Circles are natural givers. Sometimes they are generous to a fault and may give away everything they have if others need it!

Just like all the other shapes, Circles come with their inherent gifts and also certain limitations. Here is a brief insight into what doesn't work for a Circle mate.

Inherent Limitations of a Circle Partner

❖ It's easy for Circles to feel excessive guilt. And sometimes they tend to transfer their guilt on to others.

❖ When something goes wrong, Circles are very quick to blame themselves first. This creates a sense of anxiety, and then they react emotionally rather than from a place of clarity and strength. Also, this constant self-flagellation sometimes puts them in a victim or martyr mode.

❖ Circles make decisions with their heart rather than their head. They are driven by sentiments and personal values rather than facts. Sometimes, their decisions may seem illogical to a Triangle or a Box, who don't subscribe to decisions based on emotions and the feelings of others.

❖ Circles love to talk about everything and are open to asking personal questions, as well as sharing aspects of their own lives. Sometimes they can get too personal, especially for a Box.

❖ Watch what you tell a Circle! Sometimes Circles can end up blurting out things that may have been told to them in confidence.

❖ When Circles want their way, they are skilled at playing on the emotions of others to get it. They know how to get what they want. Since they read people well, they have a keen sense of what to say and to whom.

❖ Circles feel emotions intensely. They can get deeply affected by the people around them. As a result, Circles tend to sulk and may often cry at the drop of a hat.

❖ Circles tend to trust people easily, which is why they can be easily persuaded to believe something that may not be true.

Have you noticed any of these characteristics in the Circles in your life? It's important not to judge them for it, and to be patient and tolerant of their natural limitations.

How to Thrive in a Relationship with a Circle

Consider a sensitive child who is quick to show their feelings. If such a child is repeatedly told that they are 'too sensitive' or 'there is no reason to be sad' or 'you are overthinking', imagine what might happen. Chances are this child will start to suppress their feelings and try to be amiable. They will start to put up a calm and pleasing exterior. The child's unexpressed feelings of sensitivity, pain, hurt, sadness, love and vulnerability will get pushed to the background and, like most suppressed emotions, will come out bursting sooner or later.

As an adult, the Circle often displays 'pressure-cooker syndrome'. Circles are often chided for their oversensitivity, open expression of emotions and warm heart. This confuses them and they try to conceal their personality, trying to appear strong—only to explode when there is a trigger.

When upset, they can get extremely scathing and hurtful. Once the trigger passes, Circles experience strong feelings of guilt, self-hate and self-criticism. It's a vicious cycle that can be quite damaging for a Circle as well their partner and the family.

Here are some wonderful ways in which you can help your relationship with a Circle partner thrive and evolve.

1. Make them feel loved

Love is the food that nourishes the soul of a Circle. Always let your Circle partner know that they are loved. Circles thrive when their emotions are acknowledged and their contribution is appreciated.

2. Communicate frequently and openly

It is extremely important for Circles to talk about problems rather than push them under the rug. Get issues out in the open and discuss them together. When Circles feel heard, they find it easier to come up with solutions and resolve issues. However, if you get into the fixing mode without adequate listening, a Circle can get cranky, angry and stubborn.

3. Remind them that it's not their fault

Circles have a tendency to get self-critical and blame themselves first. They often lack the objectivity to view issues and problems in an impersonal way. When you find your Circle partner getting drawn into the quicksand of self-flagellation, be a rational sounding board. Let your Circle know that it is not their fault. Help them build healthy boundaries and not take things too personally.

4. Be honest with your Circle

Circles are quick to trust others. Their mantra is: I will trust you unless you give me a reason not to. But once their trust is broken, it can be hard to win it back. If you do make a mistake, admit it and ask for forgiveness. Circles find it easy to forgive but hate to be lied to.

5. Learn to ignore some of the Circle's moods

Circles tend to feel emotions intensely and are prone to sudden highs and lows. If you find your Circle partner sulking or irritable, allow them some space. Don't add fuel to the fire by trying to reason with them or by asking a lot of questions. If given some time and non-judgmental space, Circles tend to bounce back faster.

6. Be willing to assume responsibility

This is especially true for major decisions at home, and particularly when family members disagree. And it's a burden that your Circle partner will gladly surrender because they do not want to feel guilty about not pleasing everyone. Also, take responsibility for financial decisions. The Circle is not skilled at this and will be pleased to be released from the burden. Keep track of small expenditures as your partner can occasionally go overboard.

7. Draw boundaries with your children

As a parent, be mindful of your children trying to get their way using emotions with your Circle partner. A Circle parent can find it hard to lay boundaries, and may not be consistent with the rules. Children quickly learn how to get their way with parents, especially if they are Circles. Such parents also have the tendency to be overly nurturing and create dependence. This can cause problems for the child in later years. Be willing to balance this out by laying firmer and clearer boundaries.

8. Encourage them to come out of their comfort zone

Circles tend to be homebodies and love spending time in their familiar zone. They can become hermits. Encourage your Circle partner to get out of the house, try new things and not get stuck in a rut. Be sure that your Circle gets enough exercise. They often tend not to.

9. Enjoy your Circle's warm and laid-back personality

Don't expect too much from your Circle. They are not ambitious and become nervous around impatient, driven or anxious personalities. If you have a Type A personality, don't expect your Circle partner to be like you.

Once you view your partner through the lens of awareness, compassion and acceptance, your relationship can become such a powerful source of joy, connection and harmony. And that is well worth investing in!

CIRCLE: How to show me LOVE

Be present to me emotionally.

Tell me often that you love me.

Be honest. I hate being manipulated.

Tell me that you appreciate me. Be specific.

Don't get aggressive with me during conflicts.

Listen to me with an open heart when I am down.

Be gentle if you decide to point out my flaws.

Take an interest in my problems.

Readily admit your mistakes.

Tell me I'm attractive and that you are glad to be with me.

Be as sensitive as possible.

16

Catch the Squiggle If You Can!

If you have a Squiggle partner, there will never be a dull moment in your life! Like the Triangle, Squiggles also have a strong personality. They are lively and spontaneous, but also mercurial and moody. Squiggle behaviour ranges from becoming ecstatic over a great new idea to total silence and deep withdrawal when things crash.

One of my clients describes his Squiggle wife as energetic and passionate, and also erratic and unpredictable. Being a Box, he finds her intense, fluctuating emotions shallow and superficial. He admires her capacity to walk the road less travelled, her appetite for risk, her ability to adapt to changing situations, her energy and enthusiasm, but also thinks she is unstable and ungrounded. Since she is impulsive, he finds it hard to trust her, and he describes her dramatic personality as incredibly exhausting.

Typical of a Box, he told me, 'She expresses strong opinions without being able to elaborate on them in detail using facts. How can I have a conversation like this?' What a classic Box–Squiggle struggle!

In my experience of working with many couples across the world, I have found the Box–Squiggle partnership very interesting and also ridden with a lot of conflicts. They are like oil and water trying to co-exist. While the Squiggle is impulsive, the Box is controlled. The Squiggle is expressive, the Box impassive. Boxes pride themselves on being realistic, while the Squiggle lives in a fantasy world. And yet, they can be wonderful together if they learn about their differences and accept each other's oddities and peculiarities. Their opposing energies can then become complementary and they can help each other grow.

If you live with a Squiggle and are not one yourself, this section will help you enhance your understanding of your partner.

Squiggle's Living Space

Home is where the heart is, and it is a strong reflection of a person's personality. Let's begin with the Squiggle's home. For Squiggles, variety is the spice of life. They get easily bored, and their homes reflect this. Squiggles like to have a different décor or theme for every room. They like stimulating colours instead of pastels, and will want whatever is in vogue at the time. Squiggles also like to have entertainment options (this is very important for them) and will invest in creating the best experience for themselves (be it the latest television, sound system, computer or even a Jacuzzi!)

Squiggles can be avid readers and their preferences can range from literature to science fiction. They are happy to gain information from different sources, like books, television, the internet or people. It doesn't matter as long as they are learning something new.

Squiggles love to have a private den, which can function as their 'room to think'. They like their living space to be open and spacious. Modern appliances and electronic gadgets are a delight for them. They tend to be futuristic in their mindset, and their lifestyle needs to reflect that.

Love for Surprises

Nothing is more draining for the Squiggle than living a routine life. It's like a death sentence! Squiggles love surprises, experimenting and exploring new avenues. If you want to thrive with Squiggles, you have to be very flexible with them and be willing to go with the flow.

My beautiful Squiggle friend Mira once wrote love notes to her husband on multicoloured sticky notes and hid them all over the house for him to find—and then forgot where she had hidden them! Once, when we were chilling over dinner, her husband said to me, 'Mira and I are completely opposite in how we feel about trying new things. I resist and often fear it, while she positively craves it. For as long as I can remember, I haven't even liked trying new foods, preferring instead to eat what I already know I like. Mira, however, almost never orders the same thing twice. In fact, when we go out, she would rather not even go to the same restaurant again. Not only that, I thrive on my predictable routine, and am perfectly happy to do the same things day after day. Mira finds routine poisonous to her passion for life. We are truly like chalk and cheese.'

Mira was listening. She added, 'Not only am I not afraid to try something new but I also thrive on it. I like the stimulation of the new. I love adventure. It makes me feel like I am alive! Otherwise, life can be so boring.' I watched them both and smiled.

Spend Now, Think Later

You need to remember to save your money because a Squiggle won't! Squiggles tend to impulsively spend now and think later. True Squiggles don't track their finances or investments. They find dealing with monthly bills and maintaining accounts boring.

Squiggles will never plan for retirement and often gamble with speculative stocks and high-risk investments. While this can pay off occasionally, it can also lead to huge losses. But Squiggles will get over it and move on!

Need for Entertainment

Since Squiggles get bored easily, they need options for entertainment. Squiggles love games that challenge the mind—Scrabble, chess, word games, riddles—especially with a worthy opponent. Squiggles can stand out in any social setting. They can be equally comfortable discussing a topic with a group of intellectuals as they would be screaming at a concert. However, Squiggles may not want to live in large families. They are not particularly affectionate or people-oriented and tend to prefer their own space and freedom.

Squiggle as a Parent

Squiggle parents can be progressive and forward-thinking. They will allow their children the freedom to experiment with ideas and encourage them to be freethinkers. Being non-conformists, Squiggle parents can sometimes swing to extremes. They can be inconsistent in laying down the rules and get dramatic at times. It's important to balance the energy of your Squiggle partner by being steady and grounded yourself.

Strengths of Your Squiggle Mate

- ❖ Excellent sense of humour.
- ❖ High energy and excitement.
- ❖ Direct and honest.
- ❖ Creative intelligence.

❖ Highly adaptable.
❖ Open to change.
❖ Life of the party.
❖ Future-focused rather than carrying baggage of the past.

Allowable Limitations of Your Squiggle Mate

❖ Moody and unpredictable.
❖ Disorganised.
❖ Trying to do too much.
❖ Sloppy personal habits.
❖ Absent-minded and mentally disconnected.
❖ Fickle in relationships.
❖ Impatient.
❖ Lack of openly expressed affection.

How to Thrive in a Relationship with a Squiggle

When you hear the term 'free spirit', what comes to mind? Maybe it's a young, rebellious child or a quirky creative adult. For me, it's the Squiggle! When you choose to be with a Squiggle, it's important to understand the core essence of this personality type.

1. Don't box a Squiggle

Squiggles don't care much about what others think of them and march to the beat of their own drum. Expecting them to live within certain societal norms will suffocate a Squiggle's free spirit. Their drive to live a life that excites them is what nourishes them.

Squiggles value experiences over objects and like to live outside of their comfort zone. They are bold, always willing to pave a new path, and take the road less travelled. They are courageous and strong-minded. It's important to acknowledge this, in order to get the best out of your Squiggle partner.

2. Freedom to be themselves

Squiggles want to be themselves, and they appreciate that same energy from the people in their lives. Authenticity is really important to your Squiggle partner. They will not put up a face to please people around them. With a Squiggle, what you see is what you get.

Squiggle partners are also intuitive and independent. While they love being the centre of attention and have no problem getting along with others, they also need their own space.

3. Naturally curious

Fear is not a big factor for free-spirited Squiggles. Not that they don't experience feelings of fear or doubt, they simply don't let these hold them back. Your Squiggle partner will always be open and curious.

Squiggles have a naturally adventurous spirit. It's part of who they are, and it is important for non-Squiggles to recognise and respect this bohemian spirit.

Here are some things to keep in mind as you successfully navigate your relationships with Squiggles.

- ❖ Keep a tight rein on the budget, as Squiggles are prone to impulsive buying.
- ❖ Your Squiggle will most likely try to squiggle out of family commitments. So, be firm when necessary. Allow them some flexibility for events which may not be that important.

❖ Get excited about their new ideas. Don't shoot them down instantly. This really deflates their spirits.

❖ Don't get sucked into their low moods; keep an even kneel.

❖ Show interest in your Squiggle partner's profession. Acknowledge the fact that they give 200 per cent to what they feel passionate about. They dream big and follow through as well.

❖ Be there for the failures. Remind them about past successes, which will give them the courage to face the future.

It is not always easy to match the enthusiasm and energy of a Squiggle. Undoubtedly, they have much to offer the world with their authenticity, independence and uniqueness. However, they can get overwhelming at times. So, here are some ways in which you can *protect* yourself in this relationship.

❖ Avoid building expectations of how things should be with a Squiggle. They will never be what you want them to be—unless that's what they desire as well. Squiggles are constantly changing. Their priorities, likes, dislikes, way of living, dreams, aspirations, views and opinions are ever shifting. So, if you try to build an idea of how they 'should' be, you are likely to be disappointed. A Squiggle is like a flowing river. There is perpetual movement.

❖ Build some permanence into your family structure. Save money, plan for your retirement, buy a house and put some roots down. Establish a steady homelife for your children. The carefree Squiggle will not do this. In fact, if Squiggles don't have continuous change in their life, they feel suffocated and get restless.

❖ Learn to draw boundaries by saying no when you want to. Squiggles can be very persuasive, especially when it comes to things that excite them and give them instant gratification. Know what doesn't work for you and state it clearly to your partner.

❖ Give your love and support without expecting an equal amount in return. While Squiggles can be sensitive and empathetic, they don't always allow themselves to feel or process their own emotions, or those of others. Develop your own support system of family and friends. Don't depend only on your Squiggle partner for emotional support.

❖ Be prepared to play second fiddle. Recognise that your Squiggle will always be the life of the party and you may be forgotten sometimes. Don't take it personally.

❖ Develop your own career and interests. Don't be dependent on a Squiggle. Your free-spirited Squiggle may find it challenging to commit to a full-time job and will constantly look for greener pastures outside the boundaries of their current circumstances. Create your own sense of security and stability.

These insights will help you tremendously in making the most of your relationship with your wild-hearted Squiggle. 'She was born to be free and let her run wild in her own way. That way you will experience the best of her.' These words of Nikki Rowe couldn't be truer of a Squiggle.

SQUIGGLE: How to show me LOVE

⌇

Give me freedom. Don't try to fence me in.

Engage with me in stimulating conversations and laughter.

Listen to my ideas and appreciate my vision.

Don't try to change my style. Accept me the way I am.

Don't tell me what to do.

Join me in my fun activities and adventures when you can.

Be excited. Show energy and enthusiasm.

Be responsible for yourself. I dislike clingy or needy people.

Don't take me personally during my periods of withdrawal.

Avoid building rigid expectations of how things should be.

Respect my varied interests and abilities.

17

How to Thrive with a Rectangle Partner

B eing vulnerable can be very unnerving; it defines who we are and how we behave. For a Rectangle who is going through an emotional upheaval, home needs to provide stability.

Rahul came to me at a time when he was suffering tremendous inner turmoil. He had been trying to establish himself in a new role professionally, but things were not working out. He was extremely frustrated at work and was struggling to find his ground. He had a strained relationship with his parents and siblings, and his lack of success was affecting his marriage as well.

This is an excerpt from one of our coaching conversations:

Me: Rahul, you have been suffering from a lot of fatigue lately, haven't you?

Rahul: Yes, it's terrible. I'm not sleeping well, and I can't get through the day without feeling exhausted. It's overwhelming.

Me: Tell me more. What's going on?

Rahul: Work has been incredibly challenging. I was quite successful at my earlier role, but now I am really struggling. My boss is very demanding and critical, and that makes matters worse. It feels like every area of my life has been affected. I have withdrawn from my family. I don't feel like reaching out to my friends. I really need support from Gina [wife], but she is also very irritable. It's extremely difficult.

Me: That sounds hard ...

Rahul: Yes, it is. Most people around me don't seem to understand what I am going through. I can't handle any more pressure. I know Gina is also struggling with my mood swings and indecisiveness, but I can't seem to help myself.

Me: At this moment, what do you need from people around you, especially Gina?

Rahul: I just need her to be patient with me. I need her to believe in me. I need to know that I matter to her, and that she loves me and respects me. I just need a supportive environment where I am not judged or criticised.

Me: It seems like you need a space where you feel loved, supported and free of pressure ...

Rahul: True. This is a transition phase and I know it won't last forever. But there are moments when I feel like I am unable to cope. I feel confused about the best way to deal with situations and doubt my own abilities. That's the time when I seek reassurance and support, especially from people close to me.

While Rahul eventually found his mojo at work and is doing extremely well now, this phase was very challenging. In our sessions, Gina understood that Rahul was going through a Rectangle phase and learnt how to support him. This, in turn, helped Rahul move through a trying period with more ease and clarity.

Living with a Rectangle is not an easy task. You need to go the extra mile to understand and adjust to the needs and vulnerabilities of your mate. It is important to remember that life's transitions can be difficult because they force us to let go of the familiar and face the future. This can make the Rectangle feel fearful, anxious or uncertain.

This section will give you some insights into how you can create an ideal environment for your Rectangle partner.

1. Conversations Are the Key

Encourage your Rectangle mate to speak. When Rectangles talk about their issues and feelings, they gain more clarity. Ask a lot of questions, listen with compassion and acknowledge their feelings. Don't try to fix your Rectangle or give them solutions too early in this process.

Intensify your love and support. Try not to be too critical, even of obvious mistakes. It may be tough for you, but your Rectangle needs it. Also, be sure to create your own support system of friends and associates. You will also need to care for yourself at this time. And your Rectangle mate may not be in a position to do so.

You should try and focus on the fact that, even if things are bad, this is a transitional phase and it will pass. But when they are in this phase, your Rectangle partner will need your support more than ever. If you stand rock solid and give care unquestioningly, when this entire experience is over, you will have an incredibly healthy and positive relationship with your partner.

2. Keep It Simple

Do not clutter your Rectangle's already spinning mind with more choices. Keep it simple. Be ready to take on the responsibility of making important decisions, as Rectangles can be extremely indecisive. Keep the environment pleasant and free of pressure. Avoid making any large investments or expenses during this phase, as Rectangles can be impulsive and regret the decision later. Be prepared to keep a tight rein on the budget and control the chequebook. I have known many Rectangles who have made some bad business decisions and investments in this phase, which have cost them heavily later. They are also prone to unnecessary spending, hoping that it will help solve their problems, but it rarely does.

One of my colleagues shared an incident with me. Her husband was going through a significant Rectangle phase. They had just bought a new house and were dealing with a cash crunch.

She would tell me about the endless books her husband bought and the online courses he signed up for (many of which he did not complete), hoping it would help him. All of this put a lot of pressure on the family finances. One day she got to know that he had signed up for an expensive training programme and was planning to travel internationally for the workshop. 'Where is the money going to come from?' she asked in exasperation. He had been influenced by a friend's recommendation to impulsively sign up for it. This led to a huge fight between the couple, which took weeks to resolve.

3. Keep It Light

Many Rectangles become so dissatisfied with themselves that they complain and grumble and forget to look at the brighter side of things. You can help by keeping your sense of humour intact. Don't take the severe mood changes personally. It's never about you. The Rectangle already takes life too seriously, so it helps if you can keep things light.

If possible, take a calm and relaxing vacation. This helps the Rectangle release some of the pressure and take some quiet time for reflection. Seek new recreational outlets and do things that the both of you don't often do. This serves as a pleasant distraction to the problems and fulfils the need to explore and to experience new things.

When I went through my Rectangle phase, I joined a salsa class, a cooking class, a spiritual community, a yoga class and a trekking club. It stopped me from feeling helpless, wallowing in self-pity or spending on things I didn't need.

4. Seek Help, If Necessary

Rectangles can occasionally plummet to severe lows. If you feel your Rectangle is about to go off the deep end, seek professional help immediately. People often try to cope with everything themselves, creating greater trauma in the long term for their partner as well as themselves. Do not ignore any signs of depression, excessive anxiety, persistent negative thoughts or physical illnesses.

Seeking help at this time is the strongest thing you can do. Also, Rectangles tend to be accident-prone during this period because their thoughts are scattered and many suffer from tension headaches, backaches, digestive issues and other ailments. Some Rectangles also suffer from insomnia, so do check that your partner is getting enough sleep during this period.

5. Be Flexible

Rectangles change their minds at a moment's notice. For example, you decide to go to the movies on the weekend. You plan a fun-filled, exciting evening, followed by dinner. This could be a much-needed break for the both of you. When you suggest this plan to the Rectangle, they may be extremely excited and even grateful that you thought about it. On Sunday afternoon, the Rectangle could get triggered by something and the mood might shift suddenly. Your Rectangle who was excited about the plan may suddenly go cold, irritable and unresponsive. The only thing that can help you cope with these erratic shifts is patience and flexibility. It is helpful for you to anticipate last-minute changes and always have a backup plan ready.

6. Protect Your Rectangle

During this changing phase, Rectangles can be extremely gullible. People could take advantage of them. A confused and stressed Rectangle might believe anything at this time and end up making changes or commitments that are ultimately harmful. You may need to protect your Rectangle from getting involved with the wrong people.

Here is a case in point. My cousin was keen on starting his own business. He came from a family of professionals (his father was an accountant, his mother a teacher and his sister a doctor) and was always encouraged to have a steady job. After working for 11 years, he decided to take a leap of faith and launch a training company. His wife was earning a stable income, which was enough to support their basic expenses.

Since he did not have enough experience or knowledge, he began by reaching out to people who had some experience in the field. One of his 'mentors' offered to come on board, provided my cousin paid him 'mentoring' fee. The mentor agreed to share his contacts and help my cousin get clients. He also asked for a percentage of the business that would ensue from such a collaboration.

My cousin agreed, and the mentor then suggested taking on board a marketing and a digital consultant as well. He suggested two names and vouched for their skills. Trusting him implicitly, my cousin went on to hire them.

For the next 12 months, my cousin paid steep salaries to

them, with no new clients or any training business whatsoever. The mentor kept making promises which my cousin, who was desperate to see his venture succeed, readily accepted.

Seeing their hard-earned money go down the drain, my cousin's wife ultimately confronted the mentor, only to discover that he and his aides had no intention of supporting this start-up. He was just looking to make a quick buck, taking full advantage of my Rectangle cousin's gullibility.

While she swiftly put an end to this, the whole episode really hurt my cousin's self-esteem and confidence. He went back to his job, but I know a part of him still hurts because of the bad choices he made.

One may be inclined to believe that the Rectangle phase has a lot of limitations and no strengths. That is far from the truth. In fact, the Rectangle phase is considered the doorway to change. Rectangles can be immensely courageous and empathetic. They know what it feels like to be caught up in a vulnerable state and tend to be very sensitive towards others who are struggling. The Rectangle phase is inevitable, and it can lead to beautiful opportunities for growth and fulfilment. When your partner moves into the Rectangle phase, it's also time to rejoice in the new unfolding, even if it comes from the deepest wells of pain and loss.

Some Strengths of Your Rectangle Mate

- ❖ Willingness to experiment and try new things.
- ❖ Searching, learning and growing.
- ❖ Sudden, unpredictable spurts of energy.
- ❖ Caring, empathetic and supportive.
- ❖ Inquisitive and willing to listen.
- ❖ Courageous and accepting of change.
- ❖ Playful and spontaneous.
- ❖ Surprises: some will be good, some bad.

Allowable Limitations of Your Rectangle Mate

- ❖ Mood swings.
- ❖ Confusion because of which they ask a lot of questions.
- ❖ Indecisive and unsure.
- ❖ Erratic, last-minute changes.
- ❖ Critical of others (especially when they are dissatisfied with themselves and the situation).
- ❖ Preoccupied with self.
- ❖ Forgetful.
- ❖ Can experience fatigue and frequent minor illnesses.

Changes are an inevitable part of life. Our brains need time to adjust, no matter the life event we're going through. If this period of adjustment is filled with judgement, criticism, unwanted advice and blame, it can feel traumatic. This is what keeps the Rectangle stuck in that phase longer. It is important to help Rectangles build their self-esteem, acknowledge their feelings, become aware of their capabilities and take a step forward. Appreciation is food for the Rectangle's soul. It's crucial to let them know what they are doing right, rather than focus on all that is wrong.

Sometimes, Rectangles can also get caught up in a negative thinking cycle. What they need is help with soothing the uncertainty that's causing their brain to fire its stress responses. Remind them that uncertainty simply means you don't know the future, and the future can be filled with possibilities.

When Rectangles greet uncertainty and the unknown with self-care, self-love and support, you and your family have a much better chance of maintaining your mental health during major life changes, and finding your way to a future that holds many new adventures.

RECTANGLE: How to show me LOVE

Be patient with my confusion and unpredictability.

Give me plenty of compliments. They mean a lot to me.

Cheer me up a little when I am feeling low.

Help me learn to love and value myself.

Respect my need to find meaning and direction in life.

Be patient with my indecisiveness.

Don't be critical of me, even of my obvious mistakes.

Don't judge me for my anxiety.

Reassure me that everything is okay between us.

When I doubt myself, remind me of my past accomplishments.

Try not to overreact to my overreaction!

18

The Art of Communicating
Despite Differences

At the core of all successful relationships is the willingness to compassionately communicate with your partner.

Most relationships fail because people don't communicate their needs and feelings in a respectful way. Partners inflict trauma on each other in the process of getting the other to listen to them.

While discovering differences is the first step to creating healthy relationships, communicating despite the differences is the more crucial second step that people need to learn.

On the long journey that couples walk together, things can get occasionally difficult. The elements that draw two people towards one another at the beginning of a relationship—physical attraction, common interests, personality connections, socio-economic backgrounds—become less central as the realities and demands of day-to-day life set in.

Over time, a couple's expectations of each other in the relationship change, and they begin to get irritated, critical and resentful. The couple unknowingly transitions from 'what *we* want' to 'what *I* want' in the relationship.

The first question I ask couples when they come in to meet me is, 'What brings you here today?' The response is almost always the same: 'We have communication issues. I don't feel understood. We can't talk about anything without arguing or fighting.'

Communication is truly the lifeblood of any relationship. We are constantly communicating with each other, whether we are aware of it or not. Literal words aside, we unconsciously communicate through non-verbal cues like facial expressions and body language. We communicate through the tone of our voice and through our behaviour. Whether it's managing conflicts, working on relational growth or intimacy, communication is the key.

Understanding your partner's inner world and having them understand yours is pivotal to true connection. If your current communication technique doesn't help your relationship evolve, then you will grow apart over time. And sometimes things get so damaged that it becomes difficult to bridge the distance.

A woman once wrote to me:

I am writing to you, as I feel like I have hit a wall and I don't know what to do. I am hoping you will be able to help me. Since the last two years, I've been having a difficult time in my marriage. Recently, my emotions have been more negative than positive, and I am starting to feel really lost and heartbroken.

'I do love my husband, but I just can't talk to him. Every time I get angry or upset, he tells me that I am overreacting or being unreasonable. I just don't feel heard and because of that I don't react well. It's a vicious cycle. I often find myself screaming and shouting to get heard, and when that doesn't happen, I break down and cry. I know that my husband loves me. But we can't seem to find a way to communicate anymore.

'Lately, he has been very distant and detached. I feel like he has pushed me away. I can't express myself anymore. I am devastated by this. Can we still make our relationship work?

This question is a common one as the two halves of a couple find the distance between them growing to such an extent that they can no longer hear each other. The fact is that each negative conversation leaves hurt and disappointment in its wake, impacting subsequent discussions. Couples could end up carrying the negative residue of a badly handled conversation in the past and use it as a weapon to defend themselves at a later stage.

'You said this ...' 'You did that ...' 'You did not even ...' 'How could you!' are statements said with intense indignation as couples try to get themselves heard. But at what cost?

I have observed a couple of things that are always at the root of a communication breakdown in relationships, irrespective of the shape of the partners.

1. Being Caught in an Emotional Storm

When emotions are running high in a relationship, each person wants to express their own point of view rather than listen. There is a pressing need to be heard and to be understood, and almost no capacity to be open to another's feelings or needs (which may be different from their own).

This leads to a situation where there is constant interruption, a tendency to exaggerate your point of view, correcting the other person—all in an attempt to control the outcome of the conversation and make sure it's in your favour.

The unconscious objective is to get the other person to agree with what you are feeling and needing. But when both partners are fighting to be understood and validated, how can the conversation go anywhere? It is bound to break down, isn't it?

Has there been a time in the recent past when you have felt emotionally overwhelmed? How has that impacted your conversations with your partner? Have you been caught in the cycle of attacking or defending your point of view but never reaching anywhere?

2. Is It Always Right to Be Right?

I am sure this has happened to you. You are talking to your partner about something important. Disagreement emerges. Your voice gets louder. You try to correct the other person's point of view. The other person pushes back. So you enter into an even longer argument to get them to understand what you are trying to say. You keep going at it till the person says, 'You are right.' Sometimes these conversations can go on for hours or days.

When you prove that you are right, it can feel exhilarating in that moment, like you've taken a drug. But here is the catch— when the effect of the high wears off, you might realise that the cost of being right is immense. The damage that is inflicted in the process of needing to be right is often difficult to repair. The other person might be left with intense anger, pain or resentment. How can healthy connections ever be possible from this space of pain?

Most people I know, including me, are obsessed with proving themselves right. Very few people feel safe enough to accept that they are wrong, especially when they are feeling intensely vulnerable.

The only way to have more meaningful conversations is to know that there is always another perspective, and everyone is operating from their own version of reality. At the end of the day, it doesn't matter if you are right. What matters is, at what cost have you decided to be right?

In relationships, we have a choice at every point. When you decide to take responsibility for your part in any relationship, ask this one key question: Do I want to win and prove my point, or do I want to develop a deeper connection and grow closer to my partner?

When couples come to me for a session, I constantly find myself saying, 'OK, now the ball is in your court. You can respond by saying something just to prove your point at the cost of disconnecting with your partner, or you can say something that will show the other person that you are willing to be open and compassionate. Connection or disconnection is in your hands.'

3. The Blame Game

When it comes to placing blame in a relationship, it's almost always easier to see faults in the other. One of the problems with couples pointing fingers at each other is that usually both parties are right, and both are wrong. Each person has an opinion of how things 'should' be based on their own needs and preferences.

An introverted Box will almost always blame an extroverted Squiggle for being too impulsive and ungrounded. A sensitive Circle will frequently accuse an aggressive Triangle of being too self-centred and insensitive.

When we blame the other person in an attempt to defend ourselves, we actually push them away, resulting in a communication breakdown. We can become so entrenched in our own argument against the other that we fail to remember that our partner is not the same as us. The more we argue for our position, the more stuck we are in our own point of view, and the less likely we are to see things from a different perspective.

We use criticism, sarcasm, labels, judgements, hitting below the belt, attacking, stonewalling and defensiveness to protect ourselves. We believe that someone or something must change externally for us to feel better. The focus is then on controlling what's happening outside than managing our own thoughts and feelings.

An important question here is this: Is it possible to completely avoid a communication breakdown? The answer is no. All relationships have conflicts and strong differences. It's not conflict in itself that creates problems; instead, it is how a couple deals with differences that can make or break their relationship.

To put love above winning and to create a space for the possibility that your opinion may be wrong, to restore warm feelings, to strengthen your relationship, to argue less and to give up the need to prove your point can literally transform the quality of your relationships. This is true: what you give out is what you get back. So when you choose love and kindness, you reap the benefits in your relationships.

HOW SHAPES THINK

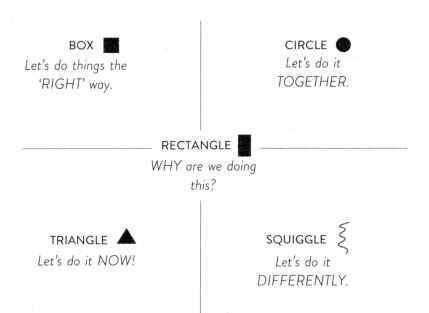

BOX ■
Let's do things the 'RIGHT' way.

CIRCLE ●
Let's do it TOGETHER.

RECTANGLE ▮
WHY are we doing this?

TRIANGLE ▲
Let's do it NOW!

SQUIGGLE 〰
Let's do it DIFFERENTLY.

19

Relationships Don't Come with a Manual

Some things are considered as part of the natural progression of life. One of them is finding love and being part of a committed relationship. According to psychologist Erik Erikson, this an important stage in our psychosocial development. His theory indicates that an emotionally healthy adult has the ability to experience true intimacy—the sort that makes it possible to have a good marriage or a genuine and enduring friendship.

While this is a wonderful milestone, the ability to sustain a healthy relationship is a different kind of challenge altogether. Nothing really prepares you for it, much like what is said about parenthood. Your expectations rarely match the reality of everyday living. Dealing with a person who has a different personality, dissimilar life experiences, unconscious beliefs, early traumas, psychological patterns and conditioning tests your patience, empathy and awareness on a daily basis.

Many of my clients tell me that they wished there was a dos and don'ts manual for creating healthy relationships. While loving another person is such a dynamic and potent experience, and one that cannot be captured in an instruction manual, I have put together a list of some dos and don'ts that could, in my experience of working with clients who come from diverse backgrounds and with very different expectations, help you manage your relationships better.

Shaan and Maya had been living together for five years when they came to meet me. I began our session by asking them, 'So what brings you here today?' This question was met with complete silence. A couple of minutes later, Shaan said, 'We have reached our wits' end with the relationship. Nothing seems to work. We argue for hours and it's taking a toll on our life in a big way. I don't think we can carry on like this.'

Maya instantly retorted, 'Don't speak for me! While you may have reached your wits' end, I know that I have been really trying hard to make this relationship work. Even seeking therapy was my idea. What have YOU done to make this work?' she yelled.

Turning to me, she continued, 'He refuses to understand what I need or make any changes. It's so frustrating. We argue for hours, but I feel like I am up against a wall. Nothing seems to get through to him. He is extremely adamant and insensitive. I am willing to walk a mile to make this relationship work, but he is not willing to even take a small step!'

Shaan sat there in resentful silence. Over the course of five sessions, I watched Shaan and Maya make some classic mistakes that erode a relationship, irrespective of which personality shape you are. They did this without realising that these mistakes were not helping them meet their needs and were instead shutting the other person down.

Here is a list of things you never do when communicating with your partner:

1. Being Too Critical

The number one destructive habit is using criticism to get your way. Criticism is a violent act and is designed to slay the other person. It is most often packaged in 'you always' or 'you never' statements. Criticism is aimed at a person's character, not their behaviour. Not surprisingly, this kind of attack tends to trigger defensiveness and leads to a cycle of conflict that is hard to escape.

Every time Maya criticised him, Shaan refused to engage in an open conversation. He would attack her back in an attempt to shut her down and gain the upper hand. This led to a vicious cycle of mudslinging, withdrawal, anger and helplessness.

In our conversations, I taught them how to take responsibility for what they really desire in the relationship. It could be as simple as starting your sentences with 'I wish' or 'I would like if you ...' instead of 'you never'. These small things made a big difference.

2. Shouting to Be Heard

The second destructive habit is yelling to get the other person to listen to you. Every relationship has its ups and downs. But screaming and yelling when things aren't going your way induces a primal 'fight or flight' response in your partner.

In her frustration, Maya tended to raise her voice. She was desperate to be heard, but it was counterproductive. Shaan reacted defensively or critically when yelled at. That defensiveness triggered more frustration in Maya, and she reacted by lashing out. Without knowing what to do or how to respond differently, the cycle kept repeating, and both partners suffered and struggled. Shaan said that he was filled with dread every time Maya wanted to 'talk'.

To break this cycle, I urged Maya to verbally acknowledge her willingness to break the pattern. It sounded something like this: 'The last time we discussed this I did not react effectively. I am going to try some new behaviours. I'm starting to feel like I want to yell, my frustration is building. I would like to stop for a few minutes so that I can get calm again.' This transformed Shaan's reaction as well and he became more open to listening without getting defensive.

3. Being Brutally Honest

The third thing that erodes communication in a relationship is brutal honesty. Being open and honest is a virtue and essential for authentic communication. Trust, which is the foundation of a healthy relationship, is also built on honesty.

Brutal honesty, on the other hand, is when someone says exactly what they think, unfiltered, no matter whom it hurts. In a relationship, when you take pride in being honest even at the cost of kindness and compassion, it can be incredibly hurtful to the people around you. It can cause your partner to go into their shell and, therefore, cause the relationship to erode. This is especially true between Triangles and Circles. Triangles believe in giving it straight, hurting Circles very deeply in the bargain.

Honesty that is delivered with a bit of compassion and kindness fosters better dialogue and leads to stronger, healthier relationships. So, if you have something to say, make an effort to do so kindly, with your partner's feelings in mind, especially if you are with a Circle or a Rectangle.

In the relationship I mentioned earlier, Shaan prided himself on being honest and direct. He believed that sometimes tough love was important. Being authentic and calling a spade a spade was his mantra. Maya felt demeaned and cornered as she listened to his scathing views and opinions. What followed were hours of arguments where Maya tried to defend her point of view. These usually ended in tears. The conversations they were having led nowhere and just heightened their feelings of helplessness and resentment.

In our sessions, we spoke about the fact that being honest has nothing to do with being angry, hurtful, mean or 'letting off steam'. Even though those emotions are not related to honesty, for some reason, we make the connection between them.

Being honest is about being more clear, more specific and

more authentic. This means that you don't have to raise your voice to show how honest you are being. You do need to be more mindful about stating your views as your own (and not the general truth) in a compassionate way and then being open to another perspective.

4. Assuming Your Partner Will Read Your Mind

Many couples (especially those who have spent many years together) expect that their partner should be able to read their mind, without they having to ask or explain what they need or feel. People want their partners to intuitively know what they are going to say before they do.

This can be extremely tricky. Your partner's mental and emotional world could be very different from yours. Your needs and preferences aren't the same either. A dominant Circle can never truly understand a Box's need to remain logical, especially during trying times. A Triangle may find it hard to understand the confusion and internal turmoil of a Rectangle. A Squiggle may erroneously believe that the rest of the world is as free-spirited as them and wonder about the boundaries of a Box.

Over the years of working with hundreds of couples, I have realised that expecting your partner to guess what you need (or don't need) and how you feel is an absurd assumption that only leads to misunderstandings, disappointments and arguments.

During the course of our sessions, I heard Maya say, 'I feel so upset with Shaan. I shouldn't have to tell him _____', or 'He should have known that this would be important to me.' Or Shaan would say, 'She should know that I am not okay with _____.' Both subconsciously believed that the longer they were together, the less they would need to explain. This expectation was never met and caused a lot of frustration.

The only way partners can get their needs met, their desires understood and their dreams acknowledged is by expressing them clearly. These desires must be shared gently. None of us is entitled to having our needs met just because we are in a relationship. While it's wonderful when our partner truly 'gets' us, this cannot become a demand that has to be met no matter what. Because nobody can understand you all the time.

There is so much more peace in a relationship when partners don't have such expectations. It's best to express yourself at the right time in a truthful and loving way.

5. Not Trying to Repair Matters When Things Go Wrong

Conflicts are inevitable in relationships, and their roots lie in our personality differences. In the quest to get our needs met, we may sometimes end up hurting our partners. Those traumas accumulate over time and threaten to insidiously damage the relationship. But is it possible to completely avoid conflicts? The answer is no. Regardless, conflicts are not the problem. It's how you deal with it and what you do after a conflict that matters. As long as couples are willing to admit responsibility for their part in the problem and realise their partnership is more important than the issue at hand, they will keep growing in their relationship.

The goal is to understand what went wrong, be willing to listen with an open heart and make your next conversation more constructive. This willingness to repair any hurts or wounds creates a closer emotional bond between two people.

Shaan and Maya learnt to repair their minor emotional injuries, and avoided creating baggage of unresolved anger or pain. They told me about a time when they were planning a weekend getaway. Maya had prepared well for this trip, and while she was busy with the last-minute details, she expected Shaan to load their bags in the car. When she finally came out, Maya saw Shaan busy on the phone and the bags still inside the house. This is when Maya 'completely lost it', as she put it, and started shouting at Shaan, labelling him insensitive. Angry tears and loads of accusations followed.

Rather than responding to Maya's distress, Shaan reacted by getting defensive and neither said a word during the entire drive.

As they recounted the incident in my office, Shaan explained that Maya had never asked for his help in preparing for the trip. Maya responded by saying that she shouldn't have to ask for it in the first place! It turned into a back-and-forth debate as each person argued for their own subjective reality.

I then guided Maya to express what she really felt when she saw Shaan on the phone. Maya tearfully said, 'I got upset when I saw him on the phone. Deep down, I felt like the trip wasn't important to him, that I wasn't important to him. I really need to feel like I matter.'

Shaan looked confused and said, 'You matter to me more than anything.' This statement reopened Maya's heart. It was like fitting the right key into a lock.

In a subsequent conversation, they both spoke about what was really happening without accusing each other. Shaan told her about his fear—that he had miserably failed her in their marriage and that he was responsible for her unhappiness. As they spoke about their insecurities, pain and vulnerabilities, the chasm between them didn't feel as wide.

While conflict did create damage, this conversation helped to repair it. Emotionally healthy couples don't shrink away from conflict; they use it as an opportunity to learn and grow. What matters the most to them is to make an attempt to reconnect and repair after a tough conversation. Otherwise, a couple can end up with layers of pain and resentment from years of unresolved conflicts.

A couple once asked me, 'You have told us everything we mustn't do. So what do we do then?'

Here is a brief list of things you must do when communicating with your partner:

1. Respect Each Other Despite All Your Differences

Learn to respect your Box mate's solid dependability, the Triangle's ambition, the Circle's sensitivity, the Squiggle's creativity and the Rectangle's courage.

As you fall in with the daily routine of a relationship, it becomes easy to forget your partner's inherent strengths and focus solely on limitations. In lasting, healthy relationships, partners value each other and the gifts they bring to the bond. Even differences are expressed with dignity and compassion. If you hope to be respected, give that same respect to your partner, day in and day out.

2. Express Appreciation

One of the great maladies of strained relationships is the lack of expressed appreciation and affection. While Circles do this naturally, the other shapes may need some reminding. All of us have been guilty of taking our partners for granted at times. If you can regularly remind yourself how lucky you are and how valuable your partner is—and tell them so—your relationship will go the distance.

Partners who share a healthy relationship regularly appreciate each other. Recognise what your partner is doing and let them know that you're thankful for it. Every day.

3. Learn to Let Go of Old Hurts and Grudges

Squiggles are good at moving on; Boxes are not. We are all different people, and our differences are bound to trigger our partners. A Box partner's logical approach to problem-solving can trigger an emotional Circle, just as a Triangle can get annoyed with the Squiggle who has a strong mind of their own.

Despite all your awareness of differences, there will be times when you feel hurt in the relationship. The key is to forgive, let go of grudges and start over each day. While this is easier said than done, letting go is crucial to the long-term health of the relationship. The past resentments you hold on to work as poison that will erode the very core of your bond.

4. Strive to Stay Calmer During Disagreements

What damages a relationship the most in the course of disagreements is how quickly arguments turn nasty. Extensive research conducted by relationship expert Dr John Gottman has shown that couples who become hostile very quickly during disagreements are far more likely to break up. Nobody wants to live in a war zone or feel like they are constantly walking through a minefield.

Interestingly, when a partner makes a deliberate effort to remain just a little calmer during a tense conversation, they usually find it easier to communicate. Despite that, there will be times when arguments spiral out of control. It's important to know when to stop and take time out, so that you can cool down and recover before you go back to the conversation. It is easier to take a pause before communication breaks down than to repair the hurt from a discussion after it has gone bad. Our brain is built to remember the nasty things that were said, so be mindful of your words and your tone, and the impression it can leave on your partner.

5. Consciously Nurture Your Bond, Every Day

In the routine of daily life, it's easy for everyday tasks to take precedence over building a bond with your partner. When someone puts a lot of their attention and energy into their relationship regardless of the million other things they have to do, it doesn't go unnoticed. Triangles cherish the warm support of Circles and Squiggles love the small, thoughtful things that Boxes do to show their love and care. A Rectangle is forever grateful to have a Circle partner who acts as their cheerleader. When done mindfully, acts of love can build an immensely strong and meaningful connection.

Understanding each other's needs and preferences, ensuring your partner feels heard and understood and practising small acts of kindness every day can help build a strong bond even when life's stressors get in the way.

6. Be Emotionally Present

Just being physically around each other every day is not the same thing as being emotionally present for your partner.

Being truly present in another person's life means involving yourself in their hopes and dreams and taking the time to notice what really matters to them. By expressing your desire to know and understand your mate, you can make them feel like you're both on the same team.

Ultimately, the quality of our relationships dictates the quality of our lives. When relationships are happy and meaningful, it impacts us at every level—physical, emotional and mental. And we could have control of all of this.

20

I'm Not Mad, I'm Just Stressed!

As a mental health practitioner, I have spent years not only learning the subject but also gaining insight into my own behavioural patterns and emotional issues. I was a traumatised teenager grappling with a full-blown identity crisis. Often, I felt lost as I tried to figure out my place in this world. I could list with incredible speed all the things I was not good at but could not remember even five things that I really cherished or valued about myself.

As a youngster, I asked myself with alarming regularity: 'What's wrong with me?', and often felt hopeless and overwhelmed. Those of you who have ever felt this way know that the anxiety of not fitting in can be quite crippling. Don't you think so?

Studying human behaviour opened amazing new doors for me. A light bulb went on in my mind and suddenly everything became clear. I moved from asking 'What's wrong with me?' to 'How can I make sense of what happened to me?' I could finally understand why people behaved the way they did, and why I reacted the way I did. It dawned on me that I wasn't all wrong, and neither was anyone else. We all just lacked the emotional and mental awareness to understand what was happening to us. I developed a lot more compassion towards myself and also for those who I believed had wronged me. It felt like a huge weight off my shoulders.

After a couple of years of practice, I needed a change of scene. So, I decided to take a break and work at an advertising agency for a while. I believed that a creative, glamorous and fun-filled job would do me good. I aced the interview (I can make quite an impression when I want to!) and started on the job.

Two weeks into the new role and I was struggling. My boss was a dominant Triangle–Box, who ran a tight ship. An ex-army man, he expected complete allegiance, unfaltering respect for his authority and unusually high levels of discipline. He did not take kindly to anyone disagreeing with him. He thought nothing of raising his voice in front of team members, and could be quite scathing at times. He expected everyone to work long hours and worked alongside tirelessly. While he worked hard, he partied harder. Business thrived under him, but I seemed to be wilting under the pressure. People who aligned to his way of working did well at the agency. Those who didn't felt traumatised every day.

The work that I was expected to do required the creativity, spontaneity and extroverted energy of a Squiggle, and the ambitious go-getter attitude of a Triangle. Two months into the job, the Circle within me started to feel overwhelmed. Unable to cope with the pressure, I would feel a lot of anger, anxiety and frustration. I hated waking up in the morning, complained of aches and pains and had digestive issues and recurring headaches. I became irritable and snapped at friends and family far too often.

I was clinically stressed! While each one of us needs a certain amount of tension in our lives to be healthy and productive, when there is too much, it can only be detrimental. Fortunately, due to my training in mental health, I quickly recognised that this role and environment was misaligned to my personality and natural preference, and I emerged from that experience stronger and wiser.

I realised that my sensitive Circle needed a nurturing

environment to thrive. My natural need to please others made
it difficult to draw boundaries, and this led to work demands that
I couldn't fulfil on a sustainable basis. I worked best when I was
appreciated, but shrank under criticism. The fact that I wore my
feelings on my sleeve meant I got hurt regularly.

Overt and regular displays of aggression is one of the most
disrupting and unpleasant situations a Circle faces, so this power-
oriented environment disoriented me.

I knew with clarity that this was not a personal failure. Here
is a simple fact: if you want to remove a screw, you choose a
screwdriver and not a hammer. This doesn't mean hammers are
useless. They are great at driving nails. But screwdrivers work
better at removing screws.

And so it is with people. In the right environment, in the
right jobs, in the right relationships, shapes tend to thrive. But
if you choose a Squiggle to design detailed standard operating
procedures (SOPs), they are bound to get stressed and
overwhelmed. All because you chose the wrong shape for the job.

In the familial space, when my Triangle sister was expected
to be a Circle daughter-in-law, she couldn't sustain that soft,
nurturing energy for a long period. Her innate Triangle tendency
to speak her mind, take charge, draw boundaries, be independent,
have an ambitious career and make firm decisions surfaced after
a while, often in an explosive way.

Similarly, my Triangle husband gets exhausted when I expect
him to be a Circle with me. He does his best to listen and to
be empathetic to my challenges, and he tries not to fix things
immediately, but it takes a toll on him.

Getting out of our comfort zone occasionally is wonderful.
It challenges us and allows us to expand and use the strengths
of all the shapes within us. However, when one is expected
to constantly operate within one's least used shape, it can get
overwhelming and stressful.

In the next section, let's explore what stresses each shape and how it affects each of them. Why is this important? Because we tend to believe that what stresses us would stress other people too. We assume that the people we find difficult to deal with would be a challenge for others too. But this is not true in practice. Different things cause stress to different shapes. The more we understand these differences, the better we can cope with people and situations.

21

Stress and the Box

Let's do a quick exercise. Take a moment to think of a dominant Box in your life. This person could be your partner, parent, sibling, colleague, friend or relative. Then think about the significant others in the life of that person. Notice the types of people who tend to cause the Box the most and least amount of stress.

You will notice that Boxes are likely to feel most comfortable with people who are like them, and most triggered by those who have a different temperament. This is true for all shapes.

Most of us know that opposites attract and there are two evolutionary advantages to this. Firstly, when people are different, they complement each other and become a strong team, and the stronger they are, the more likely they are to survive.

Secondly, if a certain degree of difference doesn't exist between people, comfort could quickly turn into boredom, and the relationship might stagnate.

But harmoniously coexisting with opposites is not always easy, is it? That is why this section is important. You will now discover who and what causes stress to a Box. Note that not all stress is bad. Some amount of tension is healthy and conflicts can also be productive. Knowing when it's tipping over the edge is what will save your relationship.

What about Squiggles Triggers a Box

Squiggles are obviously at the top of the list of people who trigger a Box. Squiggles don't pay attention to details. Their lack of structure and disorganisation can be a major cause of stress for a Box. Also, Squiggles have a highly changeable personality, whereas Boxes prefer people who are consistent and dependable. Squiggle traits are most unacceptable to a Box at the workplace.

I had an insightful experience about this when I was working as a consultant with a pharmaceutical company. The Learning & Development manager of this company was a dominant Box. He was a perfectionist, monitored every small detail, could get critical when processes were not followed and focused extensively on trivial details of day-to-day tasks. He was always well-prepared for meetings, asked a lot of questions, made meticulous notes and expected others on the team to be as diligent as him, if not more.

Unfortunately, most of his team members were either Squiggles or Circles. They were spontaneous, creative, ideas-oriented, intuitive, highly energetic and open to changes.

Their lack of attention to details and disorganised way of working was a perfect contrast to the serious, solid, structured, dependability of the Box boss. This caused a lot of regular friction between the team and the boss. As a result, this Box boss took on a lot of work and persistently micromanaged the team. When confronted with this feedback, he said that his team did not inspire his trust. Not a surprise, is it?

What Is It about Circles That Triggers a Box

The main concern of Circles are people, whereas Boxes focus on the task at hand. At work, a Box will find it hard to understand why Circles are so concerned with the way people feel. Boxes think that people should comply with processes and focus on getting the job done. They are proficient at keeping personal and professional boundaries clear. Given their quiet and introverted nature, they find the Circles' need to talk (especially about people and emotions) very draining.

The Box boss I mentioned earlier had a team member who was a dominant Circle. She was sensitive, friendly and shared a good camaraderie with her team as well as other stakeholders. This boss, however, found it very challenging to deal with her. He believed that she spent too much time trying to connect with people rather than focusing on getting the task done. He felt that she was too emotional and excessively involved with people at a personal level, which was unnecessary.

In one feedback exercise, this junior expressed that she felt unacknowledged and unappreciated by her boss. She felt demotivated by his lack of personal connect with her.

When this feedback was shared with him, the Box boss was extremely unnerved. He prided himself on working hard and getting the job done and expected the same from others. So, what was the need to get so emotional about it, he questioned.

How Rectangles Trigger a Box

Boxes have a love–hate relationship with Rectangles. Boxes are initially put off by the confusion and uncertainty of Rectangles. However, if Rectangles come to them for advice, they enjoy the opportunity to share their in-depth knowledge and happily guide the struggling Rectangle.

Boxes can be excellent teachers when they choose to be. They are patient, structured, detailed and consistent in their willingness to support others. Rectangles can always rely on a Box for practical advice. Since they are going through a state of transition and change, this makes them most open to new perspectives. Thus, Rectangles can make ready students for willing Box teachers.

What about Triangles Triggers a Box

In most situations, Triangles and Boxes make an excellent team. They are both left-brained, analytical, logical, task-focused, know the rules and live in a structured environment.

Stress occurs when the Triangle assumes a commanding position and tries to make major changes without giving the Box adequate data or time. Unless Triangles take the time to explain the changes carefully to Boxes, they will be met with discomfort and resistance.

It is worth mentioning that a second point of struggle between Triangles and Boxes is the way they deal with conflict. While Boxes have a tendency to avoid confrontation, Triangles choose to express themselves directly. Triangles will always argue to win. They openly express their views and can be extremely imposing. Boxes, however, withdraw in the face of a conflict, and tend to keep their views to themselves. This eventually leads to pent-up resentment towards Triangles.

Having said that, the Triangle–Box combination tends to make the best team, and as long as the Triangle is the boss, they are highly productive together.

How the Box Deals with Stress

Aarya worked as my assistant for two years. The reason I hired her was her loyalty, dedication, methodical and structured approach, ability to be extremely meticulous and organised, and her need to be perfect at what she did. In short, I hired her for her Box-like traits.

Things went well between us, and soon I came to highly depend on her. Being a Circle myself, I knew a lot about Aarya's personal life. She lived in the city alone, was in a relationship with a man she adored and had a small group of close friends.

She came from an affluent family of Triangles, and always felt the pressure to perform and live up to expectations. She often felt pushed and cornered by her overachieving family to do more with her life. She was extremely sensitive to negative comments and blunt feedback.

She also got triggered when she was pushed to deliver without being given adequate time or enough data.

After a couple of months of working together, I sensed a change in Aarya. While she tended to be a loner, I sensed that she was increasingly more withdrawn. She became resistant to my ideas, forgetful and disorganised, which was very inconsistent with her Box-like traits. I noticed her mood swings and irritability. She had difficulty making small decisions and seemed unsure at times. I could see that she had not been sleeping well and was not as put together as she usually was.

It was time to have a chat with her; this was a tall order given that she was an introverted Box. But it needed to be done. Over a couple of patient and non-threatening conversations, I discovered that Aarya was dealing with significant relationship problems. Her Triangle–Squiggle boyfriend was a perfect contrast to her quiet demeanour. He was aggressive, demanding, social and fun-loving. It was challenging to keep up with his needs and she was exhausted. She felt judged for being rigid and resistant to adventure. He found her need for predictability and structure very suffocating and expressed his dislike bluntly. She preferred time alone with him and now she was forced to interact extensively with his large circle of friends. She found them superficial and loud.

Aarya was dedicated to the relationship, which meant that she wanted to make it work. But it was taking a huge toll on her and the stress was apparent.

Since Boxes are not vocal about what's happening inside of them, it's important to identify when they are stressed, so that they can be supported in the right way, at the right time.

Here are some typical signs of a stressed-out Box. Needless to say, every Box might not display all the signs, or in the same intensity.

- ❖ Disorganisation: This is a first real giveaway for the Box who is usually very organised.
- ❖ Withdrawal: Since Boxes tend to be loners, this is their natural reaction to stress. They find it hard to talk about what is worrying them and withdraw further into their shell. In a way, this is counterproductive as they need the support and understanding of others.
- ❖ Forgetfulness: An important sign of a Box in extreme stress is when they get disoriented, confused and occasionally forgetful. This is exactly what Aarya displayed when she was stressed.
- ❖ Insomnia: More than any other shape, this red flag emerges strongly with the Box, so watch out for it.
- ❖ Indecision: Although Boxes are not known to be quick decision-makers, under stress they will have difficultly even with simple, everyday decisions.
- ❖ Excessiveness: Boxes' negative traits can intensify due to stress. They can overly micromanage, nitpick, procrastinate, complain, become aloof and start to work alone. They may also start to eat/drink/smoke too much—or overdo things usually done in moderation.
- ❖ Workaholism: Because Boxes are work-focused, when the going gets tough they tend to turn up the heat and work harder.
- ❖ Depression: When stress takes over and the confidence of a Box is eroded, they may just give up and show signs of an emotional downswing. While a full-on depression is very rare, a Box may need temporary help from a professional counsellor to tide over the crisis.

Six Ways To Help Your Box Reduce Stress

1. Talk about it

This may not be easy as the Box is not comfortable talking about emotions. While Boxes may not know the exact reason why they are stressed, talking about it can help them find clarity and get to the source of stress. Stress reduction begins when Boxes acknowledge that they are tense and know the cause of it. Without this, any resolution is impossible. My discussion with Aarya led to a lot of clarity as she was able to identify four or five issues that were really causing her stress in the relationship. She could also see that her reactions were aggravating the situation rather than resolving anything.

2. Explore alternatives

Boxes have a strong left-brain orientation, so problem-solving comes easier to them, especially when it is supported with logical options. Having alternatives to deal with a situation also takes away their feeling of helplessness. Since Boxes can be resistant to change, it is important to be patient and allow the Box to come up with possible solutions rather than jump in to fix the problem or offer advice.

In my conversation with Aarya, she came up with three possible alternatives during the discussion:

- ❖ She could decide to leave the relationship.
- ❖ She could continue with the way things were.
- ❖ She could attempt to draw certain boundaries, firmly and compassionately.

We discussed the pros and cons of each option, and she eventually decided to have an open conversation with her boyfriend, expressing what she can and can't do in the relationship. She did this without being apologetic or getting triggered. They negotiated and came up with a solution that worked for both of them, at least in the short term. While it was not easy, it had to be done. This relieved Aarya's immediate stress and gave her the mental bandwidth to think more clearly.

3. Exercise

This is a proven method for dealing with stress for many people. For a Box who tends to suppress feelings, it becomes especially important. Encourage your Box to take up any solo activity that they might enjoy, like walking, jogging or cycling.

4. Go back to the comfort zone

If the source of stress is at work, let them withdraw into the comfort and support of loved ones at home. Make an extra effort to keep the environment stress-free without added emotional strain or chaos. Try to be available when the Box needs you, to talk or just for some company.

5. Get professional help

If your Box goes through a significant crisis, seek external intervention. A Box will respect knowledge, and will appreciate the advice of a professional. It is best to use this option early rather than wait till the stress causes serious damage in the form of full-blown depression or a stress-related disease.

22

Stress and the Triangle

You might wonder what stresses Triangles, considering they live life on their own terms. It turns out that Triangles are likely to have the most stressful lives, but *by choice*. They are action-oriented, ambitious and enjoy making decisions necessary to resolve crises that others may find hard to handle. They love the adrenaline rush that challenges bring. Many Triangles are happiest when there are deadlines to meet and they have some level of tension in their lives. In fact, Triangles don't particularly like it when things run smoothly. This is true both at work and at home.

Here are some fun things you must know about Triangles.

1. Triangles don't know how to lose gracefully

Try telling a Triangle 'It's only a game', and they just don't get it! They tend to be competitive because they want to be the best and hate losing at anything. They will play to win, and it doesn't matter if it's at work or in a round of cards.

2. Triangles don't know how to enjoy the journey

Triangles are extremely goal-driven. Given that they're so occupied with achieving their goals, they don't understand how to go with the flow and enjoy the journey. They are always focused on what's next. They rarely stop to celebrate their achievements before hopping off to the next challenge.

3. Triangles don't know how to sit still

You will never find Triangles enjoying a zen moment. They constantly move—shake their feet, twiddle their thumbs, grind their teeth, compulsively check their email, bite their nails, twirl their hair—to discharge their restless energy. Relaxing is not only low on the priority list, but it also feels like a waste of time.

4. Triangles don't know how to live without to-do lists

Triangles can't imagine going through their tasks without to-do lists. Recalling every task from memory is a fantasy, and Triangles are not willing to take that chance, in case they miss a deadline or a target. They dislike leaving things messy or incomplete and prefer to see all their tasks plotted out.

5. Triangles don't know how to take it easy

If you tell a Triangle to be somewhere at 6.30 p.m., more likely than not you will find them walking towards you at 6.25 p.m. Time is of the utmost essence, and Triangles don't want to waste it. Because they are impatient, speed and brevity are key to their daily functioning. They have no patience for incompetence or long explanations. They like people who can communicate quickly, clearly and briefly.

And the reason Triangles get so wound up is that they put a lot of pressure on themselves to be their best possible version.

Stressful People for Triangles

Given all these quirks and eccentricities, Triangles can find other shapes stressful and challenging, and they have no qualms expressing it. Squiggles, Rectangles and Circles—in that order—tend to get on a Triangle's nerves. Having said that, they can tolerate these shapes if they are in an authoritative position.

What about Squiggles Triggers a Triangle

Here is an important fact: while Triangles have the most dominant personality of all the five shapes, Squiggles are also equal in their personal power, especially when their ideas or sense of freedom are at stake. When a Triangle disagrees with a Squiggle's idea, sparks can fly. The Squiggle will respond tenaciously, while the Triangle will fight to win. It's a close contest!

I frequently witness this between my Triangle husband and my Squiggle mother-in-law. She is a woman of ideas and advocates for them strongly. Once she had an idea of investing in a holiday home. She spoke to a couple of people and was inspired to create a getaway space where she could take a break and have a blast with her friends. Over dinner that night, she launched into an animated conversation with my husband about her new idea. It was fun to watch this exchange between them:

Mum: I'm so excited! We need to buy a holiday home now.

My husband: (*impatiently*) So what's this new idea now?

Mum: I was speaking to a couple of people and everyone seems to be investing in a holiday home. Imagine how much fun it would be to have a getaway place!

My husband: Yes, I know. This has always been on my agenda....

Mum: (*interrupting*) My friend was saying that there are some new properties coming up. I think we should check them out and pay the deposit. Almost everyone I know has a holiday home now. We would have so much flexibility to go any time and stay for a longer duration too!

My husband: (*logically*) Of course not. I have already thought about it and I have bigger plans.

Mum: (*now upping her excitement*) Those can happen later. We can always upgrade, can't we? Right now, let's start with this holiday home. I am already imagining my weekends away. I have so many friends who would be delighted to come. We should buy a place that has more rooms and an indoor pool as well ...

My husband: (*irritated*) Mom, investments don't work like that. They need to align with a long-term vision. Investing in the first thing you see is irrational. It simply doesn't make sense. You are always excited about a new thing, insist on it and lose interest just as quickly.

Mum: (*now angry*) You always shoot down my ideas. You think you know best, but I always have good ideas. You just don't want to listen. Anyway, I don't need you to agree with it. I can do what I want.

My husband: Fine, go ahead. I don't agree with it, so I won't be doing any of the legwork, negotiations, paperwork, etc. You can do whatever you want. In any case, you will forget about this in a couple of days and then there will be a new idea. I know you, Ma.

Mum: Forget it. One day you guys will realise what you are missing in life and then regret it. You just don't value my ideas. (*Dramatically rolling her eyes*)

My father-in-law who is a Box and I (a Circle) sat in amused silence as we waited for this squabble to end. Squiggles get excited and move from one thing to the next, which can drive Triangles crazy! Triangles are the most focused of the left-brained shapes, and Squiggles are the *least* focused of the right-brained shapes. That in itself is a huge cause of contention between the two.

What about Rectangles Triggers a Triangle

Triangles dislike people who don't have their act together. People who don't have clarity, confidence or competence, or who tend to come across as unsure or confused, do not have Triangles' respect. They have little patience for people who don't know their mind or don't share the same level of conviction as them. Rectangles tend to feel unsure and overwhelmed, and that can make taking decisive action very difficult. This can really trigger a laser-focused Triangle, who can start to sideline them.

On the other hand, Triangles love to lead, and the Rectangle is a prime candidate for that. The Rectangle is most susceptible to being swayed by the Triangle's powerful and dominant personality. Once Triangles see that they can manipulate Rectangles, the stress vanishes.

How Circles Can Trigger a Triangle

Triangles are sure to have significant Circles in their life. The empathetic and warm-hearted Circles balance the sharp edges of the Triangle. They are more tolerant of Triangles' high-strung nature, which most people find hard to deal with. Circles are easy-going, forgiving and relaxed, which works in favour of hyperactive Triangles. Circles are there to remind Triangles to unwind and be mindful of their tendency to take too much on their plate.

Problems emerge when the long-suffering Circle partner who has sacrificed their own needs in the relationship to accommodate the powerful Triangle starts to feel resentful. Triangles can stress over a situation where Circles make them feel guilty about all that they have sacrificed.

Being a dominant Circle, I find it easy to sidestep my needs in favour of my Triangle husband's. His energy, competitive spirit, time urgency and tendency towards workaholism can all be very exhausting to the normally relaxed and laid-back Circle in me. Instead of voicing my objection, I would often go along with him and overlook his irritable outbursts. But this came at a cost. A couple of months into the marriage, I started to quietly seethe about always having to be the accommodating one. I would not feel heard or held when I hit my low moments. I started to make frequent comments about how I was always the one expected to understand, and insisted on detailing the extent of my sacrifices. That made my Triangle husband extremely uncomfortable. He felt guilty and angry about it, till one day he pointed out to me that he never asked me to sacrifice my needs (which was true) and it was my choice to do so.

Another aspect of the Triangle–Circle conflict occurs in the work setting. Circles tend to get excessively involved in the lives of other people, whereas Triangle are focused and task-oriented. They find the Circles' sensitivity unnecessary, which can sometimes be an impediment to taking charge and getting tasks done. Triangles complain about Circles bringing personal problems to work and expecting them to be sympathetic about it. If the Triangle is the boss, they can put a stop to this and make a Circle's life miserable in the process. This is not intentional; the two merely have different objectives at work.

How Boxes Can Trigger a Triangle

Usually, Boxes and Triangles can coexist harmoniously. The problem occurs when Boxes get stuck in the details and are not able to match the Triangle's pace. The Box's need for information and perfection can be annoying for Triangles. For them, achieving results is of prime importance, and there is always a time urgency attached to that. They find it hard to deal with the Box's commitment to the 'right' process and sticking to the tried and tested.

My Triangle husband finds it excruciating to deal with some Box clients. When on call with a Box client, he has to consciously slow down his pace and suppress his need to talk about results quickly. He struggles to be a good listener. It's amusing to see him grit his teeth, tap his foot or drum his fingers as he tries to answer the long list of questions that the Box invariably has—and sound sincere in the process! It's excruciating for him to elaborate on the 'process' that will be followed to achieve the results, and also talk about past data to support his view.

But he does all this exceedingly well as my Triangle husband has his eyes set on the goal (which is to the win the trust of the client), and he will do all that is necessary to get there.

Signs of a Stressed-out Triangle

Here are some typical signs of a stressed-out Triangle. It is important to remember that every Triangle might not display all the signs, or with the same intensity.

1. Anger outbursts

When a Triangle feels out of control or has taken on more than they can handle, they tend to fly into fits of rage. Rather than retreat, the Triangle will express anger towards others. That is when you know that the Triangle is stressed and you need to get out of the way!

2. Hyper-critical

This is a nasty side-effect of a stressed-out Triangle. It is normal for a Triangle to be blunt and direct without worrying about the consequence. However, stressed Triangles tend to berate others for their failings or perceived shortcomings, and their inability to live up to the impossibly high expectations they may have of them.

3. Frequent colds/flu

Since Triangles lack the ability to calm themselves down when stressed, their body tends to be susceptible to illnesses to a greater degree at this time. Most people can tolerate some level of stress and chaos, but Triangles have a higher threshold. In fact, Triangles can work harder when stressed, hoping to get back in control, which adds to the pressure on the body. This leads to chronic exhaustion, headaches, digestive issues and much more.

4. Avoidance

During stressful times, we all need a robust support system of friends and family. But Triangles don't allow themselves that. They tend to avoid friends and family and withdraw into their shell, especially when they feel they are up against the wall. This is because they are too proud to admit vulnerability. Triangles don't want others to see that they are not in control because they don't want to lose the respect of those people.

Once my Triangle friend had a severe bout of a viral infection. It caused painful rashes and blisters all over his body. But he did not reach out to anyone for support, despite having a large network of colleagues and friends as well as family. He was single, lived alone in a high-rise apartment and had limited access to external support. When I asked him why he did not ask for help, he simply shrugged it off and said he could handle it, and it was not a big deal.

Six Ways to Help Soothe the Stressed-Out Triangle

When you are living with a Triangle, there are some things that are a given. They are impatient and irritated as they tackle multiple things at once, often without a break.

They wear stress almost as a badge of honour. Most Triangles speak rapidly, eat and walk quickly, tap their foot or drum their fingers when waiting, click their tongue or grind their teeth and heave sighs of annoyance. In my conversations with many Triangles, I figured they don't even realise how hyperactive they seem to others.

While stress can help Triangles achieve their goals and push through a tough situation, if left unchecked, it can affect their physical and mental health in the long run. Here are some ways in which you can help the Triangle in your life reduce stress.

1. Watch for early warning signs

Since most Triangles fail to recognise that they are stressed, you need to watch out for excessive anger, irritation, fatigue, insomnia, frequent illnesses or withdrawal. The greater the frequency and intensity of these signs, the more important it is for you to intervene in time. Do not take their aggressive behaviour personally. Being patient will help you maintain your sanity in the process.

2. Change of environment

Just getting away from a routine, even if for a short weekend, can work like magic to soothe the frenetic Triangle. If that isn't possible, ask them to take short breaks throughout the day to breathe, talk with a friend or enjoy a cup of tea or coffee—all of which can be calming. Find out what helps your Triangle mate to soothe themselves and create space for that.

3. Make time for exercise

Insisting that your Triangle takes 20 or 30 minutes every day for any activity that gets their heart rate up can help reduce stress and improve their mood. It could be walking, a session at the gym or any other activity that the Triangle enjoys.

It took a lot of cajoling for my Triangle spouse to take out time for strength training and swimming sessions three to four times a week. Though he resisted intensely, I put my foot down on this one. While he continues to check his email in between workouts, this routine provides an outlet for his pent-up energy, releases feel-good chemicals and puts him in a better mood for the rest of the day.

4. Connecting with old friends

It is always nice to connect with friends who were a part of the Triangle's life before it all got so hectic. Reunions can be wonderful for them. Meeting up with friends after a long and stressful day at work can help the Triangle blow off some steam. It is important to remind your Triangle partner that being a workaholic can isolate them and aggravate stress, while having a few supportive people to talk to can work wonders.

5. Redirect their energy

Triangles have a lot of restless energy. Ask your Triangle to get involved in some project that is outside their work environment. This gives them a sense of achievement without the stresses associated with work deliverables. They also get an opportunity to broaden their scope of activity, connect with different people and have non-work conversations.

When the COVID-19 pandemic hit, my Triangle colleague

was going crazy at home. All his travels came to a standstill and he was like a caged animal. That's when he started directing his energy at home, micromanaging things, controlling and commanding people. Unable to deal with this, his wife called me and said that she would leave him if he continued to drive everybody crazy at home. One evening, I suggested to this Triangle colleague that there were several groups that were focusing on getting medical supplies for critically ill COVID patients. This project needed someone who was focused, aggressive, well-networked and unwilling to accept no for an answer. This profile was a perfect fit for my Triangle friend if he would be interested.

He got involved with one such group and did a stellar job of it. Eventually, his contribution was acknowledged at the national level and it gave him a tremendous sense of accomplishment. This redirection of his energy also saved his marriage.

6. Teach them to trust others

Triangles have a great need to be self-sufficient and work hard to retain their independence. However, some level of dependence is natural, especially during times of crisis. Triangles don't like to feel vulnerable and try not to depend on others emotionally.

But during times of stress, they need someone they can talk to. Triangles need to learn to rely on others, and you need to help them create that support system.

Like Boxes, Triangles place a lot of emphasis on accomplishing tasks required at the workplace. Unlike a Box, the Triangle wants to be in charge of those tasks and achieve results. This can make them extremely driven, and the Triangle doesn't know when (or how) to slow down. The debilitating effects of stress could creep in before they are recognised.

If you happen to be the person a Triangle trusts, it is important for you to encourage them to relax. It may be difficult, but Triangles must learn to listen, unwind and rely on others for their own good.

23

Stress and the Circle

C ircles and Boxes have one thing in common when it comes to stress: they are both least likely to show it. This, however, does not mean that they do not experience it.

Circles are easygoing people who take life as it comes. They are more stable as compared to Squiggles or Triangles. You will rarely see a Circle in a hurry. They enjoy what they do and take their time. Their lives are relatively calmer. Even if they get behind on something, they don't worry about it much. Circles don't feel the need to compete with other people, and tend to be more satisfied with their life.

Though Circles have fewer stress triggers, they certainly experience significant anxiety when it comes to relationships and conflicts—be it personal or professional.

This section is especially important if you have a Circle in your life and need to know what to expect when they are stressed.

Stressful People for Circles

1. Boxes

Boxes (not Triangles) are the number one stressor for Circles. The reason is simple: Boxes are practical, not prone to expressing their emotions or displaying affection. They can seem serious, cold and aloof to the warm and affectionate Circle. Boxes thrive on respect and not love. They need consistency and structure, while Circles function best when there is flexibility.

In a way, Boxes are quite the opposite of Circles. They prefer to not mix business with pleasure, whereas for Circles there are no clear boundaries. A Circle may make lot of effort to get close to a Box, and get them to open up, but Boxes take their own time to build comfort and trust. When a Circle fails to build a close connection with a Box, they can feel rejected and hurt, and might eventually get resentful towards the latter.

I once had a Circle client, Adhira, who was married to a Triangle, and had a Box mother-in-law. Adhira made an effort to blend in with the family and take care of everyone's needs. She once told me, 'I lost my mother when I was very young. I never got to share my love with her. Marriage has given me another chance to experience the love of a mother.' But her mother-in-law was not a Circle, and would not reciprocate her emotions in the same way. While she openly expressed her affection, her mother-in-law preferred to keep her distance.

Adhira felt immensely hurt and rejected by this, and spoke about it often in our sessions. When she tried to share this with her Triangle husband, he immediately got to problem-solving. He suggested that she should not be 'oversensitive' as his family was generally not prone to displaying emotions.

Eventually, her mother-in-law was diagnosed with Alzheimer's disease, and Adhira took care of her. When I spoke to her after her mother-in-law had passed on, she told me that she knew the older woman really valued and respected her, but could never express her affection openly through either words or a hug, and that vacuum would always remain within her.

2. Triangles

After Boxes, Triangles come in a close second as highly stressful people for Circles. While Triangles can be extroverts and connect well with people, it's usually for different reasons. Triangles are interested in others only to the degree that people can help them, while Circles are genuinely interested in others and seek deeper connections. In short, Triangles tend to use people as a means to an end, which Circles find despicable. A Triangle boss may not take the time to ask about a team member's well-being and whether they have the bandwidth to take on new assignments. The Triangle boss doesn't request, he demands. The Circle in the team can feel very cornered and overwhelmed. But the Triangle boss will also know how to pull the Circle's emotional strings when needed, in order to get the job done.

Triangles are usually blunt, direct and comfortable with confrontations. A Circle might end up feeling judged, misunderstood, attacked or criticised. It is usually in the Circle's best interest to not be too sensitive or take things too personally, but to be thick-skinned and insightful enough to recognise that this is just the way Triangles function.

Circles tend to have a lot of personal information about colleagues and friends. Their warm and empathetic nature makes it easy for others to open up to them. They are excellent listeners. People tend to tell a Circle things they do not reveal to the impatient Triangle. But Triangles have a way around that. They tap into the emotions of a Circle and find out the latest gossip about people. Triangles then use this information to their advantage as and when needed. When a Circle discovers that they have been betrayed, it can be heartbreaking for them.

3. Squiggles

Circles recognise and appreciate human differences, so the Squiggles' eccentric behaviour doesn't bother them much. Having said that, Circles can get a bit uncomfortable when Squiggles experience mood swings. Also, Squiggles thrive on change, stimulation and new experiences. They are not necessarily focused on being sensitive to emotions or showing care and affection. This can trigger a sensitive Circle who seeks depth in connection and in the quality of relationships.

Squiggles are also not the best listeners. When a Circle needs to vent, a Squiggle may not be the best person to create a loving and compassionate space. Also, they tend to be flighty and may not be available when Circles need them for support. It's best for Circles to avoid building any expectations of consistent emotional care from Squiggles.

4. Rectangles

The remaining shape, Rectangle, is no problem for the compassionate Circle. Confused Rectangles are, in fact, a delight because they give Circles an opportunity to nurture, support and guide someone less sure than themselves. A Rectangle also makes a Circle feel needed. This allows the Circle to believe that they are making a difference in another person's life.

To sum it up, if a Circle is married to a Box or a Triangle, some adjustment is required on the part of both partners to make the marriage work. The Box needs to learn to be more expressive of their feelings and the Triangle spouse should be sensitive and compromise on some aspects that are important for the Circle.

It can be a bit rough in the beginning till both partners find their ground in the relationship.

Signs of a Stressed-out Circle

Here are some typical signs of a stressed-out Circle. It is important to remember that every Circle might not display all the signs, or with the same intensity.

1. Sullen/Quiet

Circles are generally talkative and one can always feel their warm energy. They are genuinely interested in others and find it easy to strike up a conversation. In fact, relationships are the lifeblood of Circles. When stressed, Circles become the opposite of their open, chatty selves. They become sullen, irritable and withdrawn. When you see a Circle being abrupt, moody or curt with someone, you know something is wrong.

2. Preoccupied with self

When stressed, Circles tend to overthink. They become preoccupied with their thoughts and emotions and tend to lose their connection with others. Despite being excellent listeners, they tend to get distracted and lose focus in a conversation. This is quite an anomaly for the friendly Circle who always places emphasis on being present for others.

3. Experience guilt

When Circles feel stressed, their first impulse is to blame themselves. They ask themselves, 'What did I do wrong?', leading to strong feelings of guilt, anxiety or shame.

Circles find it hard to maintain their objectivity and look at the facts of the situation. They become self-critical while doing so.

I have met many Circle parents who experience lots of guilt, anger and shame when their children are in trouble. I once worked with a Circle parent whose child was battling severe depression. The parent was caught in such an intense loop of self-blame and remorse that she couldn't provide the child as much support as they needed. During a conversation, she broke down and told me, 'I'm the worst mother ever. I never do anything right. This is all my fault.'

Circles forget that not everything is their fault, and that this kind of thinking is not helpful as it sabotages their ability to cope with a situation rationally.

4. Martyr syndrome

Circles paint themselves as victims when they are in a stressful situation. They get bitter and express it by complaining.

In a stressful situation, they have a hard time communicating clearly or directly, and expect others to guess what they might feel or need. Circles might think like they have made a lot of sacrifices (which is usually out of their own choice) for a partner or other loved ones and feel angry or dissatisfied when they don't receive acknowledgement, appreciation or gratitude in return.

Nadia was going through a stressful phase in her marriage. She had left her job to care for her two daughters. Her Box husband was unable to offer her the emotional support and connection she needed to feel happy in the relationship. She found him incapable of understanding her emotional world and, over the years, she turned resentful.

During one of our sessions, her husband requested her to share her feelings and she replied, 'It doesn't matter. If you knew me well enough, you would have also known what upsets me. If I have to spell out everything, there is no point in this discussion. It's best not to expect anything from you as you don't get me anyway.'

The husband looked at me and said, 'This is what she says when I try to talk to her. I believe that the best way is to give her space and not pursue the matter much. Am I wrong?'

Circles can also direct their anger inwards, in which case they may try to hurt themselves or may eat and drink too much to numb their pain.

5. Incessantly talk about problems

When Circles feel stressed, they want to constantly talk about their problems, which is quite unusual for a Circle who is mindful of the needs of other people. When Circles are overwhelmed, they try to make sense of their feelings by talking, especially to someone who offers a sympathetic ear. They do so in the hope that by expressing themselves they can relieve some of their pain.

This is what happened with Zubin, a sensitive, articulate man with two young children. His wife was threatening to leave him because she felt he was not ambitious enough. Zubin spoke continually for an entire session, almost without taking a breath, before I was able to interject. He said that the uninterrupted expression of his emotions helped him feel lighter.

When patience wears thin for those who listen to the rants of a Circle, the unhappy Circle will seek out new ears. While doing so doesn't solve the Circle's problem, it certainly makes them feel better in the short term.

6. Withdrawal

This is usually the last stage of stress for Circles. At their lowest point, Circles will shut down and withdraw from everyone. Insomnia, lack of energy, day-time fatigue, crying spells, anxiety, irritability and uncontrolled emotions are some other side-effects. This is the time for stressed Circles to immediately seek professional help.

How to Help Your Circle Reduce Stress

It can be stressful for us to watch our loved ones suffer from heightened periods of stress. It can be especially upsetting when the stressed-out person is a Circle, who is possibly the psychological glue of the family—the affectionate sibling, the loving friend or the compassionate team player at work. Perhaps the most difficult part is that while we desperately want to help, we often feel unsure about the best approach.

There is, after all, no one-size-fits-all method for what to do when the Circle in your life is stressed. But here are some practical tips for how you can help.

1. Listen with an open heart

The biggest fear of a Circle is being judged. Therefore, the best gift you can ever give a Circle is compassionate, non-judgmental listening. What does this mean? It is listening without judgement or the need to offer advice.

This can be deeply healing for stressed-out Circles. When Circles know that they can talk about what is happening to them, and that they will be heard, they are sure to be okay.

2. Encourage the Circle to express anger

This is very difficult for Circles because they want everything to be pleasant and don't want to offend others. Circles work hard to avoid conflict and maintain harmony. Overt expressions of anger can lead to disagreements, which makes Circles anxious. But feeling and expressing anger is a necessary stage that Circles must pass through, especially when they are experiencing stress.

Usually, Circles tend to deny or suppress their anger. They push down unpleasant feelings and continue to portray a friendly demeanour. This comes at its own cost.

For years I was unable to express my anger. With so much suppression, there came a point where I couldn't even feel it anymore. When people asked me, 'Are you angry?', I would instantly respond, 'Who, me? Not at all. Why would I be angry?' It was okay to feel sadness or fear, but anger was completely rejected and considered a deal breaker. Did that mean I never felt angry? Of course, I did, and at times intensely so. But I kept it all inside.

One day I woke up and, as usual, rushed to work. I was handling multiple projects and had a busy day ahead of me. I took a coffee break at 11 a.m. and reached out to my partner (now husband) for a quick chat. As I was speaking, I found him staring at my face. Self-consciously, I asked him why was he looking at me like that. In a quiet voice, he said, 'Your face looks strange. Why is your coffee dribbling down from your mouth? I think you need to check it out in the mirror.'

Filled with dread, I rushed to the bathroom. When I saw my partially paralysed face reflected in the mirror, my life changed. I couldn't move the left side of my face. I couldn't blink, smile or eat properly.

A visit to the ENT and a neurologist confirmed the diagnosis of Bell's Palsy, a form of facial paralysis. It was agonising to not have clarity on whether I would recover fully. Work came to standstill, meetings were cancelled, workshops were postponed, travel plans changed and counselling sessions were put on the back burner as I tried to make sense of this new development. The steroids I was prescribed were making me nauseous and I had hit rock bottom emotionally. I spent all my time in bed, staring at the ceiling, wondering why this had happened to me. I already had digestive disturbances and deficiencies due to lack of nutrient integration in my body. I often grappled with low energy and bouts of anxiety.

It then hit me with blinding clarity. The anger I had been

suppressing had become somaticised, causing ailments in my body. As Louise Hay says in her bestselling book *You Can Heal Your Life*, the mind and body are closely connected, and unresolved emotions do find a way to create physical disharmony.

My suppressed anger paralysed the authentic expression of my true feelings, and this manifested in my body. Holding back angry feelings had created tension, which played a major role in the physical condition I was experiencing. Being a pleasant and loving Circle had come at a huge cost. This awareness changed my life.

I started to notice how Circles tend to internalise feelings of anger, which causes them to turn against themselves and become self-critical.

When the anger gets too much, they see others as culprits. The supressed anger eventually explodes and they end up hurting the very relationships they were trying to protect in the first place. What results is a vicious anger–guilt–sadness cycle, which is hard to break out of. Most Circles will deeply resonate with this.

Anger is a natural response to frustration or stress, and Circles need to be encouraged to accept and talk about it. This helps them move towards positive self-expression and to avoid internalising pain or indulging in passive–aggressive or manipulative behaviour.

3. Be an objective sounding board

Circles tend to be overly emotional and subjective. They need the balance of a cool, rational friend who can be a good sounding board. When a stressed-out Circle talks to you, it is immensely helpful to acknowledge the emotions beneath the words, such as hurt, doubt, anger, self-blame or fear, and ask questions without judgement or criticism. Be cautious and gentle, so that Circles feel safe sharing their emotions with you. The idea is not to give advice; rather, help the Circle feel heard and notice something they are not seeing.

4. Reinforce positive qualities of the Circle

Circles tend to be really hard on themselves, especially when stressed. Reminding them of the things that make them special can be therapeutic. Even a simple smile or a gesture that says, 'I care about you' matters a lot.

One of my clients, Aaron, a research and development director at a pharmaceutical company, arrived at our coaching session feeling completely distraught. 'Something happened at work today that I can't get out of my mind,' he said. It turned out that Aaron had to give feedback to a colleague about a communication error, which had caused tension within the team. Aaron had spent a lot of time thinking about how to give the feedback without hurting the sentiments of his colleague. He reviewed the facts, drafted his talking points and logged on to a virtual meeting ready to have an open conversation.

Then, things went askew. The colleague got extremely defensive and Aaron struggled to be heard. At one point, the colleague got aggressive and confrontational, which put Aaron on the back foot. The conversation ended on a bitter note.

Afterwards, Aaron was preoccupied with the incident, and he couldn't stop beating himself up about how the conversation had turned out. Should he have been more sensitive? Or more assertive? Should he have used different words to convey his message? Was he too harsh? Why did he have to overexplain instead of sticking to his talking points? Why couldn't he handle it better?

His innate sensitivity and thoughtfulness caused him to spiral into self-judgement, overanalysing the incident, ruminating over the details of the conversation and assuming fault.

I reminded him of the times he had been sensitive to the needs of others, successfully supported the team and received wonderful feedback for it. We also spoke about the positive intention with which he walked into this conversation, and his attempt to have a collaborative discussion. Once his anxiety settled, he was able to look at the conversation much more objectively, treat it as a learning experience and figure out how he could have dealt with it better.

5. Be available

When the Circle in your life is stressed, be available for them. It means a lot to a Circle to have the freedom to reach out to you as and when needed. Circles usually find it difficult to ask for help, because they are natural givers but reluctant receivers.

They also have an innate fear of being rejected or considered a burden. As a result, Circles may not openly ask for support. So be the 3 a.m. friend who the Circle can reach out to without feeling obligated, and they will really value you for that.

6. Seek professional advice

If the Circle does not respond to your support and continues to remain withdrawn, anxious or low, this is definitely a red flag. Don't wait too long before suggesting they seek professional help, as such a low phase exacerbates their emotional and mental health.

Remember, your love and support for a Circle during stressful times will be repaid to you many times over. When the stressful period has passed, your Circle will continue to be generous and loyal. You cannot find a better friend than a Circle. Invest in this relationship, you will never regret it.

24

Stress and the Squiggle

Squiggles seek stimulation. As long as they have freedom and variety, they tend to thrive. Squiggles need to have lots of things going on in their life to be happy. They simply cannot survive in a boring environment. When things get dull and mundane, it puts Squiggles in a zombie-like state, devoid of their characteristic energy and aliveness.

Ayan, a strong Squiggle, lived independently and was the creative director at a media company. His work allowed his Squiggle energy to find complete expression and he loved what he did. Travelling over the weekends, having friends over, exploring new places, experimenting with food and taking up artistic adventures defined Ayan's life.

His girlfriend (a dominant Circle) lived with him along with his dog, a gorgeous Golden Retriever, and things were working quite well for them. One day, Ayan received a call that his mother had suffered a massive stroke. She was a single parent and lived in their hometown, a couple of hours away from the city. Ayan rushed to the hospital to be by her side, and within a couple of days it was clear that she had lost control of certain muscles, and would need constant support. Given the situation, his mother needed to be shifted to the city, so that Ayan could attend to her needs.

Over the next couple of months, Ayan's life went through a massive transition. His free-spirited self was now replaced by the order, structure and practicality that would be best suited to a Box. He couldn't travel like before and his day assumed a kind of mundane routine. He had to attend to several medical needs that cropped up on a daily basis. He couldn't take up new assignments that would require him to put in late hours or be available at short notice. He couldn't find the time or the will to cook, socialise or pursue his adventures. He felt caged.

His girlfriend found herself grappling with his constant irritation. He would make random plans of a biking trip to the mountains, a meditation retreat or deep-sea diving lessons, which never worked out. The more he tried to break free the more he felt boxed in.

When he came to me, Ayan had withdrawn into a shell and turned unusually negative and critical. He had lost his sense of humour and spent most of his time in front of the television, which was very unusual for this life-of-the-party Squiggle. He had become withdrawn and reclusive.

It was clear that Ayan was extremely stressed. Squiggles are creatures of extremes. When Squiggles are stressed, they can either become very outgoing and dramatic and seek to do wild things never done before, or have long periods of time in which they will not see or talk to anyone.

As with other shapes, stressed Squiggles will reveal their most negative traits. They can become sloppy, disorganised, impractical, unrealistic, illogical, uninhibited and extremely dramatic.

There are predictable stages that Squiggles go through when they experience stress. Once you know what these stages are, you will be in a better position to spot them as they happen, and will be able to support the Squiggle in your life to proactively work through the stress.

Usually, Squiggles are chaotic, hyper and full of energy, so it is difficult to recognise when they are stressed and not coping well. You need to be extra mindful to recognise the downward spiral. There are four stages Squiggles will go through when they are stressed.

Stage 1: Find an Escape

When Squiggles become aware that they are stressed, they will first try to solve the problem by changing the situation. They will change jobs and cities and find new activities or a new relationship to escape. While this might work in the short term, it rarely solves the problem. Squiggles continue to carry the mistakes, issues or residual emotions to the new situation and soon reach a dead end.

Sometimes, Squiggles can keep flitting from one thing to another till a dramatic event occurs and they are forced to face the situation.

In Ayan's case, he initially tried to cope with the situation by gaming. He would come back home after a stressful day of managing work and other demands made on him due to his mother's medical condition, then would sit in front of the gaming console, hoping to get transported into an alternate reality. This worked well for a short period, but started to create issues in his relationship and his physical well-being. Slowly, gaming got replaced by passively watching television.

Stage 2: Increase Stimulation

When this change of situation doesn't work, the Squiggle will try to find extra stimulation, hoping that it might help. This is where the Squiggle can get a bit eccentric. Sources of stimulation for the Squiggle are not your usual dinner, date night or a movie, but something radical, such as skydiving, an adventurous road trip,

Sufi whirling meditation, impulsively getting a pet, an unplanned trip or anything that provides a shot of adrenaline.

But this can provide only temporary relief. Once the high of the stimulation wears off, the Squiggle will feel stressed again.

Stage 3: Withdrawal

When Squiggles realise that nothing seems to help, they will start withdrawing. While this not a problem if it is not done in the extreme (but Squiggles are creatures of the extreme), it starts to become a challenge when they lose interest in everything, and go for long periods without seeing or talking to anyone. This phase is definitely a red flag, indicating that they need help.

Stage 4: Depression

You know it is serious when your Squiggle is depressed. During this stage, Squiggles are listless, unanimated, lack energy, lose appetite, complain of aches and pains, turn sloppy, get severely disorganised, are forgetful or have no interest in taking care of themselves. Professional help at this stage is a must.

The question that is probably on your mind is: Who/what stresses the usually laid-back, happy-go-lucky Squiggle? The simple answer to this is: A mundane life devoid of new experiences. If there is nothing exciting and challenging in their personal or professional life, the Squiggle feels trapped. They then subconsciously end up creating drama in their existing life. This is a fact that many Squiggles may not readily admit.

Stressful People for Squiggles

1. Boxes

It is obvious that Boxes are number one on the Squiggle's hit list. Several times in my counselling practice, I have mediated between Box and Squiggle spouses. The issues are usually the same. The Squiggle wants to travel, the Box wants to stay at home. The Squiggle wants to try out new things, the Box prefers to stick with the tried and tested. The Squiggle desires change, the Box likes familiarity. The Squiggle wants to challenge status quo, the Box wants to maintain tradition. The Squiggle wants to experiment, the Box wants the comfort of predictability. The Squiggle feels suffocated, controlled and limited by the highly left-brained, organised, practical and disciplined Box. The differences are enormous and can lead to significant clashes.

Even at work, the Squiggle needs autonomy and freedom to try out new things. They hate being stuck in a rut and thrive best in changing and challenging environments. Squiggles do not adjust well in bureaucratic companies. They are not detail-oriented and consider paperwork a waste of time.

They flit from one idea to another, and may not even pause to see the idea through to fruition. All this can be extremely annoying for the Box. If the Box is in an authoritative position, this can become a major source of stress for the free-spirited Squiggle.

One of the reasons my Triangle–Squiggle husband became an entrepreneur is because he had a Box boss. After business school, my husband took his time to decide on the organisation he would work for. It was important to him that the work culture be able to support his innate need for autonomy. He zeroed in on a job profile that required an independent thinker. He was interested in roles that allowed him the opportunity to design new systems, explore different locations and work in a results-driven environment.

While he found such a role, he had to report to a Box boss. This proved to be really hard for him. He felt intensely limited, micromanaged and controlled. He knew that this was the reality of the corporate world, and that he would need to tame himself and blend into the needs of the boss and the organisation.

Unwilling to let go of his natural preference, my husband eventually chose to break away and start on his own. Initially, it was a struggle, but the promise of freedom and new experiences kept him going.

He tells me that the biggest advantage of being self-employed is that it gives him the freedom to base his office anywhere he likes (the beach is his preference). He gets to choose the work he wants to take on, and there are always new challenges to look forward to. What means the most to him is the opportunity to make his own decisions and live a life of his choosing.

2. Triangles

Triangles want to wield power and impose their thoughts on a Squiggle. However, Squiggles have strong ideas of their own. If the Triangle is in a position of dominance, it can become stressful for the Squiggle.

Triangles are extremely focused and goal-oriented. They work with the end result in mind, and relentlessly pursue it. This is quite different from the Squiggle, who is a person of ideas. Squiggles are essentially right-brained, creative, spontaneous, erratic and highly changeable. Their focus is on the uniqueness of the idea, and not just the goal.

When goals have to be accomplished, Triangles can get driven, controlling and bossy, which Squiggles find hard to deal with. Triangles think of Squiggles as being indisciplined, unrealistic and inconsistent.

Having said that, I have also seen this relationship work well when the Triangle is willing to listen to the ideas of the Squiggle. After all, the Triangle can never think out of the box to the extent a Squiggle can. At times, the unique ideas of the Squiggle can help the Triangle accomplish things they would not have been able to otherwise. And that's valuable to a Triangle who is constantly looking to stay ahead in the race.

3. Circles and Rectangles

Usually, these two shapes do not pose any problems for a Squiggle. The Circle is most capable of patiently dealing with the Squiggle's eccentric behaviour, without getting into an argument. Circles are also willing to please, which works well for Squiggles.

But Squiggles tend to be self-centred (in a different way than Triangles) and find the friendly and sensitive demeanour of Circles convenient as well as appealing.

What can stress a Squiggle is when Circles get oversensitive or emotional. Squiggles are not about depth of emotion; rather they are about the breadth or variety and the expression of emotions.

Squiggles also value authenticity and honest expression of ideas and feelings. It is extremely stressful for a Squiggle when they struggle to understand the layered intention behind what a Circle does (Circles do things to please others and not because they want to). During those times, they find Circles fake.

Squiggles usually enjoy spending time with Rectangles as they are always willing to listen and learn new things. Rectangles are willing to experiment because they are testing themselves on all levels, and this works well for spontaneous Squiggles.

Like Squiggles, Rectangles also have sudden, unpredictable bursts of energy. They are playful, open to change, curious and accepting of new ideas. They both are forgetful, disorganised and have a short attention span. What works in the Squiggle's favour is that Rectangles are unusually caring, supportive and empathetic. They know what it feels like when others look at you as crazy, inconsistent and unpredictable (especially the Boxes), so they are able to be empathetic towards the predicament of Squiggles.

Help Your Squiggle Reduce Stress

Before Squiggles reach the phase of withdrawal or depression, there are some things you could do to help them reduce their stress.

Being a Circle, Vinita (Ayan's girlfriend) intuitively understood that something was wrong with him. While she offered a lot of support and love to him, she and I spoke about some strategies she could use to support Ayan's Squiggle personality even in the future.

1. Be a grounding presence

It's essential for Squiggles to trust that you truly care for their well-being. This can happen when you are available for the Squiggle as a sounding board. Squiggles need to feel safe to express their ideas and feelings with you. They must trust that you will not judge them or rush to put a damper on them. Squiggles are also highly expressive and dramatic, so you need to learn how to be emotionally present without getting sucked into their histrionics. Squiggles also tend to be moody and may suddenly withdraw for short periods of time. Do not take it personally. Once the trust builds, you will be in a position to discourage any action that you believe will ultimately harm them, and Squiggles will surely be open enough to receive your suggestions.

2. *Allow your Squiggle their time alone*

Squiggles are highly independent; they hate being smothered. They are free-spirited people and need a lot of space to be themselves. They don't want to be boxed in or feel restricted by the expectations of others.

Therefore, it's important that when you're with a Squiggle they have complete freedom to express themselves and do whatever they need to stay calm and focused. Allow them to spend time alone, engage in hobbies they enjoy and make their own decisions without feeling pressured.

3. *Don't give ultimatums*

Never tell your Squiggle mate something that has the word 'if' in it like, 'If you don't stop doing this, I'm going to leave.' Squiggles hate being cornered or trapped, be it at work or at home, and it activates their rebellious streak. They will be off and running before you know it. Giving a Squiggle an ultimatum is like caging a bird that needs to spread its wings. Don't do it.

4. *Don't get controlling or parental*

Squiggles follow their gut instinct and experiment with things. Let your Squiggle partner go ahead and make their own mistakes, even if it's hard for you to watch. Do not force your opinion on them because it would be disrespectful of their personal space and independent streak, and they'll resent you for making them feel like they don't have any choice in the matter.

Listen to what they have to say, offer your suggestions and let them make their decisions, even if you disagree. If the Squiggles in your life trust you, chances are that they will be more open to your views.

5. *Try to ensure a balance of excitement and downtime*

Like I said earlier, Squiggles are creatures of extremes. Their hyperactive personality can exhaust them mentally and physically and they may not even realise it.

My Squiggle mother-in-law needs more excitement than most people in the family. In the eagerness of all that is possible, she plans for loads of events and activities, which are beyond her physical strength. And she loves it! However, after two days of intense hyperactivity, she is completely exhausted and needs to stay in bed to recover.

Anybody who has Squiggles in their life has to realise that they will need more excitement than the normal person, but they also require quiet time to revitalise their energy.

A final note: Do not allow your Squiggle to totally withdraw as this could be the beginning of a downward spiral. Stay connected with the Squiggle, particularly if you know that they are already experiencing some level of stress.

25

Stress and the Rectangle

The Rectangle shape is stress personified. Rectangles are people who have been experiencing major changes in their lives, which brings on the stress of not having clarity and of adapting to new circumstances. Their situation consistently involves letting go of the past before they can embrace the new.

While working with thousands of people across the world, I have met several Rectangles. I have witnessed their confusion, angst, thirst for direction and hunger for clarity. I have also seen their courage, openness and vulnerability.

While some level of anxiety is a natural outcome of being a Rectangle, what one needs to be careful about is the frequency and intensity with which they feel stress.

A Rectangle wife was at a café with her husband. After several minutes of reading the menu, she said, 'Um, let's see. I don't know what to order. Maybe I'll have the burger. No, wait, actually the pasta also seems good.' After a while, she said, 'I think I should just stick to soup and salad. What are you ordering? That sounds good. Maybe I should have that? I don't know, I just can't seem to decide.'

Rectangles are a confused lot.

But if Rectangles are excessively stressed, they might find it difficult to make even small everyday decisions. They might agonise over what to do, vacillating back and forth, and constantly second-guessing themselves even after the decision has been made. A Rectangle under stress will be forgetful, distracted, unsure and doubtful. While this is a characteristic of the shape, these traits intensify under stress.

Rectangles can also display significant mood swings under stress. These emotions can emerge within seconds and can be triggered by small things, sometimes seeming to have no basis in reality. As a result of this, the behaviour of Rectangles is also unpredictable. At times, they can be a warm Circle, followed by an impulsive Squiggle or a headstrong Triangle. Because Rectangles are in such a severe state of change, they can become different people every day, and it is impossible to foresee what they will become next.

This is what happened with Gina, my friend from school. She married young and was completely in love with her husband. She had known Vishal for a very short period before she decided to take the plunge. He was an engineer, working in the R&D department of an organisation. Gina loved kids and worked as a preschool educator. She was a classic Circle–Squiggle.

Eight months into the marriage, Vishal got a posting in London, and had to move within two weeks. Gina decided to quit her job and follow him, though it was not an easy decision for her. She struggled in the new country, with no family, friends or the job that she loved. Less than a year later, Vishal was grappling with serious issues at work and decided to quit. After his two-month notice period was over, both moved back to Mumbai.

Over our customary weekly coffee meet, she spoke about how uprooted she felt and hoped that Vishal would soon settle into a job he liked.

His second stint lasted 17 months (with a lot of ups and downs) before he quit again and decided to start his own consultancy. It was a start-up and put significant pressure on their finances. They had just had a baby and Gina needed to get back to work to support the family financially.

The next three years were extremely challenging for Gina and Vishal as they coped with numerous changes and challenges. Gina had to play the role of a nurturer for the baby, the emotional anchor for her husband and breadwinner for the family.

I watched the transition as she changed from a fun-loving, generous, warm-hearted person into a struggling Rectangle. There were times when she behaved like a tough Triangle, focused on achievement and financial growth; on other days she was a detail-obsessed, micromanaging Box. There were times when she would get into the skin of a Squiggle and make an impulsive decision to buy an expensive gadget. She struggled with bouts of low self-esteem. It was confusing for people around her as she took on the characteristics of any of the four shapes at any time, and they simply couldn't predict who she would be next.

There were times when her old self would emerge, but it would instantly be replaced by some other shape, as Gina subconsciously believed that being her usual free-spirited Circle–Squiggle would not work to help keep her family safe. I knew that as long as Gina continued to reject her natural way of being, this stage would go on. And the longer it continued, the more stress it would cause.

Over time, Gina built her trust and confidence and regained her footing. Vishal's consultancy also secured some loyal clients, and the couple did not have to worry about their basic needs anymore. I knew then that Gina would now slowly step out of the Rectangle phase. She would probably never fully go back to her original self as this experience had changed her at her core, but her Circle and Squiggle would surely take the front seat again.

Stressful People for Rectangles

1. Triangles

They are the number one source of stress for Rectangles. The reason is simple: Triangles are tough, clear, confident and decisive—all qualities that Rectangles lack and want most. It's easy for Rectangles to get inspired as well as intimidated by Triangles.

Triangles get impatient with indecisive Rectangles and look down upon their confusion as a sign of weakness. Triangles respect people who can take charge, are in control and whom they can depend on in a crisis. Rectangles aren't those people. I have often observed Rectangles trying to please Triangles (who are hard to please anyway), and not succeeding at it for long. This really affects their self-esteem and puts them on the back foot.

A Rectangle client once told me, 'Whenever I try to speak to my Triangle boss, I feel so intimidated that my brain gets fogged. I lose my train of thought, fumble through my words and simply fade into the background, letting him dominate the conversation. His ability to speak his mind so effortlessly and command the crowd only heightens the feeling of my inadequacies.'

Here's another perspective: Rectangles can also have difficulty dealing with Triangles, more so if they themselves have been a Triangle in the past. Then the envy for the lost confidence is even more acute.

2. Squiggles

Though both shapes have a lot in common, sometimes Squiggles can intensify the confusion in Rectangles. Squiggles are naturally prone to jumping from one thing to another, talking about multiple ideas at the same time, deviating from the topic at hand, changing their mind often and leaving conversations unfinished, which can leave Rectangles feeling even more bewildered.

When I was going through a Rectangle phase at work, I reached out to a Squiggle mentor for some advice. We decided to meet at a café for an informal chat. I reached the venue 15 minutes before time with carefully crafted talking points and burning questions I needed to ask (I was in the Box mode that day).

This mentor arrived 20 minutes late, bustling with energy. He launched into a conversation about the exciting new project he was working on. A little while later, I gently interjected and asked him if he would like to have a cup of coffee. That triggered a conversation around why coffee makes us feel so good, the difference between good coffee and bad coffee, and the best coffee moments he'd had around the world!

Finally, we got to talking about the issues I was experiencing at work. While he heard some bits, he shared more of his personal stories, spoke about other people, about what was happening in the world, discussed changing trends in other businesses and gave me at least six ideas on how I could take my business to the next level.

We spent two hours chatting at the coffee shop and when I walked out, I called a friend and told her, 'I am not sure what just happened, but now I am feeling even more confused.' While it was a fun conversation, the numerous ideas and unstructured information left me more puzzled than before. This is typical of what can happen between a Squiggle and a Rectangle.

3. Boxes

The Box shape is where the Rectangle wants to get to. We all know about the Box's dependable qualities by now. Rectangles find it hard to have the discipline of the Box. Boxes are put off by the confusion and ambivalence of a Rectangle and can be quite judgmental about it.

My cousin, who has been a Rectangle for almost a decade, finds it extremely hard to deal with his Box father. His father insists that my cousin decide on a conventional career path and stick to it. He often advises his son, 'Success doesn't just happen. Consistent hard work is the basis of everything. If you don't focus and cultivate a routine, you will never get anywhere.' This really antagonises my cousin, who goes through almost daily personality changes. He seeks out new people, new job opportunities and new places as a testing ground to see what will eventually work for him. He is heavily influenced by his friends (who keep changing) and keenly follows his role models (who also keep changing). This obviously doesn't go down well with his highly regimented Box father.

What my Rectangle cousin says he needs the most is for his father to be open, encouraging and appreciative of him. He wants his father to be available to talk about problems and insecurities, without offering judgement or advice. This can be difficult even for a well-intentioned Box because they feel totally at loss when dealing with Rectangles.

4. Circles

The most positive shape for a Rectangle under stress is the nurturing Circle. They are great listeners and are highly compassionate towards the internal struggle that Rectangles face. Their gentle understanding can be a healing experience for anxious Rectangles, who feel unconditionally accepted by benevolent Circles.

It is to the Rectangles' benefit to seek out Circles during their transitional period. In fact, one of the common outcomes of divorce during a person's Rectangular period is the replacement

of a Triangle spouse with a Circle one! The Rectangle says, 'Now
I have someone who gets me. I feel loved and accepted for who
I am.'

5. Old friends

When people are in the Rectangle phase, they don't necessarily
remain the way they were in the past. Therefore, interacting with
old friends can no longer be as comfortable for the Rectangle.

Rectangles tend to seek out new people who don't have a
predetermined image or expectations of them, which creates
scope for experimenting with new behaviours. Also, old friends
remind the Rectangle of their past self—someone they no longer
want to be. This puts pressure on old friendships and sometimes
the damage is irreversible.

Help Your Rectangle Reduce Stress

Living with Rectangles is not easy. You need to be aware of their
state of mind to help them cope with stress.

Often when Rectangles pass through their painful period of
transition, they may look around and be surprised to see that
there are very few people left in their inner circle.

Here are some ways in which you can help your Rectangle
cope with stresses.

1. Provide constant support

My clients have been an incredible source of inspiration for me.
Here is what Saina (my Rectangle client) wrote to me after she
had passed through the Rectangle phase.

'For most of my life, I did not have much support for the
things I was passionate about. I am one of the only people in my
family who chose to pursue a career as a writer.

'In fact, I did not tell my family about my writing till a year ago. I was raised to be practical, have a stable career and live a conventional life. But it did not work for me. I felt restless, lost, confused and very unfulfilled.

'I changed jobs, tried new roles, took online classes to upgrade my skills, spoke to people, but nothing really made any sense. It only added to the confusion. It was painful and lonely as most people I met seemed so sure about what they were doing and what they wanted in life. I felt something was seriously wrong with me. Today, I realise that it was an important phase where I was redefining myself.

'What I needed the most during this phase was unconditional listening, support and acknowledgement of my struggle. You offered me that. When I came for my sessions, I felt like I could speak my mind without the fear of being judged. Your steady encouragement helped me build trust in myself. Having you by my side made a huge difference.

'For the past eight months, I have got much better at finding balance in my life. I have found my passion in writing, and have been more diligent about it than anything I have done before. It makes me happy. Things are much easier when you have someone in your life who supports you in your highs as well as your lows. I hope to be that person for the Rectangles I meet in my life. Thank you for everything you did.'

Reading this just reaffirmed to me that what Rectangles really need is your support and love.

2. Keep it light

Rectangles can take themselves too seriously, especially when they are stressed. They can get moody and edgy. Try to keep the home environment light. Laugh together, watch happy movies and surround yourself with upbeat people. This will take the edge off to some degree.

3. Encourage new and different things

The more Rectangles expand during this phase of transition, the greater their chance of getting the support and clarity they need. Encourage Rectangles to connect with new friends outside their current field of interest. This will help them try out their new 'selves' as they redefine who they are.

Encourage them to pursue different activities. This will also serve as a distraction when they get stressed.

If you sense that the Rectangle's need for change is job-related, encourage them to have an open dialogue about what is needed. If you resist the situation, it will take the Rectangle much longer to cope with the internal turmoil. You might need to shift the financial burden on to your own shoulders during this period.

4. Inform family and close friends

When people who are close to Rectangles are sensitised to their inner turmoil, they can support them better during this phase, without getting personal, defensive or irritable.

Rectangles don't need someone to fix them or their problems; they just need to know that their feelings are important, heard and valid. The fear of judgement can be a big obstacle for stressed Rectangles. Let them know that you support them and be respectful of the changes happening within them.

Final note: Be sure to reinforce your own support system of friends, family and associates during this time. I met Sasha when she was in the middle of a crisis. Her 17-year-old Rectangle son was in full-blown rebellion mode. He would come home intoxicated many nights, and on others he wouldn't even show up. As a single parent, it was incredibly tough to establish a stable, loving home environment, draw healthy boundaries and also give him the unconditional love and support he needed. Initially, Sasha was holding on by a thread. We spoke about the need to consciously strengthen her support system.

She reached out to family and friends to help her pull through during this challenging time. It amazed me to see the number of people who were willing to be there for her. A couple of months later, her son recovered from this phase, and she emerged strong and emotionally intact too.

The Rectangle phase passes. Remember that, even when things get bad. Your Rectangle friend or family member needs your support more than ever. If you remain steady and balanced, both you and your Rectangle will emerge out of this phase with a positive relationship. And that is well worth it.

26

Your Best YOU

Many of us are set in our ways.

Raj expects the house to be tidy and organised when he comes home from work. He dislikes clutter or chaos. His wife is free-spirited, involved in multiple activities and not attentive to details. He feels exasperated and she feels controlled.

Rina is a high achiever and heads a wellness company with her husband. She is laser-focused and completely driven. Her husband is creative and works in bursts of energy. He has many other interests apart from work and loves his freedom. She feels angry when he doesn't show enough ambition, and he feels belittled and disrespected for having different needs.

Avani and Tanvi are siblings, born two years apart. They share a lot of physical similarities but have different personalities. Avani is polite, practical, conventional and follows rules. She is well-liked by teachers and performs well in school. Tanvi gets easily bored, has trouble staying focused and, despite being intelligent, almost never gets good grades. She is highly individualistic, full of new ideas and hates being boxed in. Avani feels the pressure of having to be the 'good girl' of the family, and Tanvi hates being compared to her sibling constantly and expresses her deep hurt through rebellion.

Mihir is a sensitive teenager. He is warm, loving and

affectionate. He is popular amongst his friends, and the one they reach out to in an emotional crisis. He is fun-loving, laid-back and gentle in his approach to life and relationships. Mihir's father is a go-getter. He is a self-made man and extremely proud of his accomplishments. He wants his son to be strong, ambitious and a high achiever. He is often critical of Mihir's lack of focus. Mihir feels anxious as he unsuccessfully tries to live up to his father's expectations.

These are just a few of the instances I have seen of how personality shapes show up in life. We are all different from each other, yet it is not always easy to accept and live with those differences. A natural reaction is to criticise others and defend ourselves. Most people erroneously believe that they are self-aware and understand differences. While 95 per cent of people believe they're self-aware, in reality, just 10 to 15 per cent actually are, according to a five-year research project by organisational psychologist Dr Tasha Eurich.

There are two distinct aspects of self-awareness: internal and external.

Internal self-awareness is when we know our preferences, needs, emotions, behaviours and reaction patterns. External self-awareness is an understanding of how other people perceive us. Externally unaware people may have no clue how they come across to other people, and are surprised when people give them feedback.

Throughout my life, I have closely watched other people, the way they behaved and also my reactions to them. However, it took me years to realise that introspection did not necessarily mean self-awareness.

I learnt that being self-aware meant feeling a deep level of compassion towards the self and others. It meant dropping the lens of judgement and experiencing a greater level of acceptance. It was about feeling at peace with myself and with the different personality shapes that existed around me.

Another thing that crops up frequently is when people use their personality as an excuse for their behaviour. 'I can't help it, that's just who I am'—I have heard these words a million times and they are usually uttered to rationalise or justify an action, position or an attitude. In some ways, it's almost the perfect defence to any argument. When couples come to me for therapy, sometimes I hear one spouse say incredulously, 'You mean you want me to change who I am?' which makes the other person feel rotten for asking something that would help them feel better. I gently point out that change is wonderful when it helps us become better versions of ourselves. After all, relationships are meant to help us evolve and grow, right?

There's no doubt that our natural personality tendencies shape the way we feel, perceive and react to our environment. But we are not limited by those traits. We always have a choice to tone down some traits we use excessively and embrace unaccepted parts of ourselves.

Circle is my default way of being in the world. And it has mostly worked well for me. I have loving relationships, a profession that I am good at and a harmonious home environment. But when the Circle becomes excessive and dominates my interactions, I become people-pleasing, conflict-averse, oversensitive and inauthentic in my conversations. I feel guilty when I don't live up to expectations and get exhausted trying my best to always be 'up' and happy for others.

This is where balance becomes essential. All the five shapes coexist within us, and we are blessed with the ability to use all of them as we adjust and adapt to the needs of life.

When my father passed away after a brief illness, I had to take on the responsibility of winding up his thriving accountancy practice. He was a strong Triangle, who led his team of Box juniors with energy, clarity, focus and authority. He demanded commitment to excellence, offered clear directions, made sure to follow through, made firm decisions and was great in a crisis.

At home, he was my father who stood behind me as the most potent force in my life. I knew I was safe because he had my back. And he thoroughly indulged my loving Circle-ness.

A week after he passed away, I went to his office. It was extremely painful but necessary. I approached the staff with my usual Circle sensitivity and consideration. I asked them how they were feeling and acknowledged their concern about the future of the firm. I thought this was the best approach, till I realised it wasn't working at all!

They were used to the Triangle energy of my father, who led them with focus and clarity. They needed someone to take charge and give directions. In short, they needed a Triangle and not a Circle.

I went back home that night, shaken and exhausted, and knew that a new approach was needed. I cried myself to sleep, missing the reassuring presence of my father. After a restless night, I woke up tired but clearheaded. I knew what needed to be done. I took a cup of coffee and stood in front of the mirror. I looked into my eyes, and felt my internal strength, my personal power, my clear thoughts and my assertive voice. I knew I had to lead the team as a Triangle, and not hold them like a Circle. I took a long, deep breath and tapped into my innate Triangle energy. It needed to assume a stronger presence now.

For the next six months I walked into my father's office, radiating my Triangle energy. I made decisions, handled the finances, delegated tasks, identified potential talent, talked to clients, set boundaries and determined roles and responsibilities. I did this with the swiftness of a Triangle. Over time the team started to trust me, and we sorted out the business together.

You might ask whether operating as the shape most unlike me exhausted me. Yes, it certainly did. But I balanced it by allowing my Circle to take priority once I got home. I surrounded myself with loving friends and family, freely asked for hugs and openly spoke about my feelings. I truly evolved and became a stronger person from this experience.

Dr Susan Dellinger often says that being emotionally healthy is not operating out of one or two dominant personality shapes. Rather, the healthiest person is the one who can be flexible enough to use the right shape, at the right time, with the right person, in the right proportion. When this is done from a space of awareness, it puts us in control of the way we respond to situations.

Simply said, being an emotionally mature person is learning how to regulate (not suppress) your natural personality traits, so that you can respond in an appropriate manner. Using your personality as a crutch to stay in your emotional comfort zone will only limit your capability to respond well to anything you are faced with.

The Evolved Shapes

Evolution means moving towards greater emotional health and becoming the best version of ourselves. As we become more aware, we need to become less limited by the rigid structures of our personality and open up to the immense possibility of who we can be.

When we start seeing our personality as alive and dynamic, rather than just a passive system of automatic responses, we start experiencing its full potential.

How the Box Evolves

The minute a child is admitted to a regulated school, their creative spirit is 'boxed'. The intuitive, free-spirited behaviour of the child is controlled to fit into the accepted rules and norms of the education system. Here, obedience is rewarded, and rebellion is chastised. This is how the Box emerges. Some children grow out of this and find their expression through other shapes, whereas some turn into stronger Boxes.

When Boxes live many years of their life trying to create a predictable world to feel safe and in control, there comes a time when they get stuck in the rut of their own making. Many Boxes live and die in the maze of self-imposed rituals and routine. They spend a lifetime living a safe but very limited life. They never expand, reach out or try new things to add to the richness of their experiences like the Squiggle. Many of them never experience the depth of an emotional connection like the Circle, as they prefer to stay logical and avoid talking about feelings. Also, many Boxes never embrace their full power and speak their truth without the fear of confrontation, like the Triangle.

Here is what the evolution of a Box looks like. On the personal front, the true evolution of a Box requires them to become aware and embrace the need for intimacy. Although painful, it is a necessary step for a Box to become a more sensitive, affectionate and expressive human being. This evolution requires the Box to build more Circle-like traits. However, this is not easy and most of them resist. Sometimes it takes an external event like a divorce or the loss of a loved one, to trigger this kind of transformation.

Once the Box embraces the Circle within, a beautiful change occurs. They allow emotions to surface, connect at a deeper level, share their innermost feelings and become more open. Loved ones who have missed this kind of affection from them feel instantly satiated. This warmth then starts to gently smoothen the rough edges of the Box. That's when the transformation is complete.

On the professional front, Boxes need to assert themselves and operate from a space of greater personal power. Boxes are great at management, but now they need to step up as leaders. Often, Boxes continue to be Box-like although their role requires them to be more like Triangles. They often work harder, and insist that others do so too. However, working harder does not necessarily mean being smarter, more resourceful or adaptive. They tend to get stuck in the minute details of the work.

By embracing some Triangle traits, Boxes can find the courage to lead from the front.

Once Boxes develop the capacity to take a stand, get comfortable with assuming power and overcome micromanaging tendencies, they are in the perfect space to move from a position of responsibility to that of authority. That's when Boxes evolve into true leaders.

How the Triangle Evolves

Triangles have a core need for achievement, significance, power and control. And they fear they won't have it. This intrinsic motivation drives them to take charge, make swift decisions and display confidence even in the face of a crisis. They tend to be dogmatic in their views and have a strong need to be right, often at the cost of proving others wrong.

All their life, Triangles work extra hard to gain influence and win followers, credentials and awards—while looking effortlessly stylish! Underneath the surface, however, many Triangles struggle with trust, vulnerability, loneliness and lack of emotional anchors whom they can open up to. No matter how much success they experience, years of neglecting love and empathy can cause glaring holes in their psyche. In their later years, Triangles can feel an emotional void from a lack of meaningful relationships.

The evolution of Triangles can be seen in various areas of their life. As they grow older, many Triangles relax, sit back and learn to enjoy life. They hand over the reins to someone younger. This gives them the time and space to become interested in people, instead of chasing goals that need to be achieved.

As leaders, Triangles transform from being controlling aggressors to softer, benevolent dictators. They assume the role of a mentor, though Triangles always have their favourites. Their leadership style shifts from a self-centred, ambitious autocracy to a more democratic and benign style. Exhausted from so many battles at a later stage, Triangles do not seek to actively compete or confront. They are, finally, not driven by the need to win every fight. More willing to delegate, listen and be open to the ideas of others, Triangles become more effective leaders.

Status becomes less important as Triangles evolve, for they have already achieved a lot and they can now engage in social projects. For some, the political arena becomes a natural progression.

Overall, the evolved Triangle is a desirable leader, capable of making major contributions to society. Their natural leadership skills can now be used for the right reasons and not for self-glorification.

An evolved Triangle also becomes a desirable partner and family member as they display more Circle-like behaviours. Unfortunately, the children of a Triangle may now have grown up, but the grandchildren are young enough to reap the benefits of this change.

My father who transformed from an authoritarian Triangle to a milder version of himself was a delight for my nephew. I have always seen my father as a powerful protector, rather than a loving, affectionate parent. When my nephew was asked to speak about his grandfather (when he passed away) his description was that of a loving granddad who would do anything for him. My nephew remembered how his grandfather's eyes would light up when he saw him. They had long conversations, played with toys and went for drives and shopping too. I had never experienced that version of my father.

Having said that, my relationship with my father transformed as he grew older. His Circle surfaced strong as he became uncharacteristically loving, generous, caring and expressive. He urged me to chase my dreams and enjoyed listening to my stories. He loved connecting with the extended family and planned dinners and annual vacations. He became a mentor for Rectangle youngsters. I cherish those memories of my father, just as I do his strength and accomplishments.

As a spouse, the evolved Triangle tends to appreciate the contribution and sacrifices of others more. Younger Triangles can be dismissive of their partner's desire for a greater emotional connection, leaving them feeling neglected, as their ambition takes centre stage.

In their later years, Triangles often start to recognise how their relationships may have suffered and try to make amends. They become better at listening, and admit their mistakes. They learn to talk about their true feelings and express vulnerability. That's when Triangles experience greater emotional intimacy.

When my father got sick and spent a month in the hospital, my mother never left his side. One afternoon as I sat with her in the hospital cafeteria, I asked her if she was exhausted with all the caregiving. She smiled and said, 'No, I am not exhausted; in fact, I am having conversations with your father we never did in all these years of marriage. We chat into the night, and I feel the most connected with him now. He tells me about all the things he appreciates about me and admits to the mistakes he made. This acknowledgement really matters to me.' That was when I knew that the Triangle had come a full circle.

The Evolved Circle

The perspective on the evolution of a Circle is quite interesting. On the one hand, the strongest Circle traits—emotional expression and sensitivity towards people—is what Boxes and Triangles need to develop to evolve; on the other hand, these are the very traits that lead to pain and resentment for the Circle.

The numerous Circles I have spoken to, all complain about those who have taken advantage of their goodness. As the years pass, the Circle gets tired of stepping aside so that the needs of others can be met. They reach a point of intense anger towards those who expect them to accommodate their feelings but refuse to do so in return. This is when the Circle starts to transform.

It's important to remember that the biggest motivator for the Circle is to be loved and wanted. They go out of their way to support, advise and be helpful. But this comes at a cost.

Neha lives with her husband and two kids. She loves being a mother and effortlessly gives her love and undivided attention to her family. Neha spends a lot of time and energy on the people in her life.

This is what a typical day in Neha's life looks like. She wakes up, rushes to get her kids going, plans the menu for the day, checks on her husband and what he needs, makes a list of the groceries she needs to buy, calls up her mom who lives alone, makes the customary call to her mother-in-law, gets her to-do list organised and checks her phone in her spare moments.

Once she hustles the kids out of the door, she grabs a fruit along the way. While they're driving to school, Neha can't stop thinking about the text message from her sister and what she might need. She also worries about how weird her friend Priya sounded on the phone when she finally called her back. Neha had accidentally forgotten to respond to her text for over a day and now feels guilty about it.

Neha takes care of people and neglects her own needs. Her justification is: 'I'm being such a selfless mom. I'm doing so much for my partner and his family. I am the dutiful daughter, a good sister and a 4 a.m. friend. I am taking care of everybody's needs and they love me.'

This continues till one fine day she realises that people are not there for her the way she wants them to be. She feels unacknowledged, unappreciated and undervalued. That starts the cycle of hurt, which eventually leads to deep-rooted resentment.

Circles invariably feel that they've been taken for granted. A hurt Circle will blame others and get bitter about the relationship, not realising that they chose to give too much.

Circles are best known for their need to please others. Their evolution involves dissolving of the ever-giving spirit. A major shift for an evolving Circle is when they focus on taking care of themselves first. An evolved Circle starts to realise that one cannot pour from an empty cup. They develop a healthy awareness of their limitations, make fewer but more meaningful commitments and know when to act or not.

Circles start to go beyond their need for validation, accepting that they are worthy as they are. This makes the Circle immensely powerful.

At work, Circles face the resentment of juniors who want the Circle leader to take a stand, even if it is an unpopular one. When Circles do not do that, it leads to an insidious loss of respect, which must be dealt with.

When the Circle reaches a frustration point, the metamorphosis occurs. This transformation usually happens in four stages.

Stage 1: When the conventional Circle discovers that loving and caring for people doesn't give them the outcome they desire, they swing into Triangle mode as a reaction. They feel angry. They get aggressive about their needs. They openly disagree and speak bluntly. They develop a strong resistance to a different perspective and fight to be right. They lose their capacity to listen or take responsibility for their actions. While this is uncharacteristic, they feel self-righteous and justified in their reactions.

Eventually Circles realise that this approach is damaging and more exhausting, so they move to the next stage.

Stage 2: At this stage, the Circle retreats into their shell and takes on Box-like tendencies. Refusing to openly deal with the issues and collaborate on a solution, they become withdrawn. This stage is the most difficult for people who live with them as they miss the openness, willingness and warmth of a Circle. But it is an important phase as Circles get a chance to turn inward and discover their true strength. A positive outcome of this stage is when the Circle emerges with a better sense of self-worth and reduced dependence on others.

Stage 3: At this stage, the Circle starts to open up and find creative solutions to their problems. Here, the Circle might adopt Squiggle-like qualities of being dramatic while presenting solutions. They start to not care as much about what people might think of them. The Circle might also make some impulsive decisions, get rebellious and seek freedom.

Stage 4: This stage emerges when the Circle finds their ground. Although the essence of Circles remains the same, they find a new level of courage and wisdom to face problems with both sensitivity and rationality. They shed their need for approval and to make popular decisions.

When the transition is complete, Circles carry the best of four shapes!

❖ They carry genuine concern for people, like true Circles.
❖ They can draw healthy boundaries like Triangles and have the courage to make tough decisions.

- ❖ They display the emotional control of Boxes.
- ❖ They build the resourcefulness of Squiggles to work out creative solutions to problems.
- ❖ They are willing to learn, change and grow, typical of Rectangles.

It is important to note that many Circles may not reach this optimum stage of evolution. Many enter these stages, but are often sucked back into the reactivity of Stages 1 and 2, and then retreat into the familiar comfort of warm, fuzzy Circle-hood.

The Evolved Squiggle

It is only fair to say that an evolved Squiggle is highly unlikely! Once a Squiggle, always a Squiggle. It is difficult for this shape to change their essence. Remember, Squiggle is not only a personality type but also a strong way of thinking and perceiving life.

Squiggles might temporarily change to adapt to circumstances (and they can be very good at this). They can do a Box-like job from 9 to 5, behave as a loving Circle to children and make a Triangle-like argument in defence of a new idea. However, it is impossible for a Squiggle to completely evolve into another shape.

In their later years, Squiggles may experience some challenges. An old saying is very apt for Squiggles: a rolling stone gathers no moss. The constant movement of Squiggles from situation to situation means that they don't horde much as compared to their peers, who may value consistency over crazy, risk-taking ventures. This could be the security and savings of a Box, the achievement and accolades of a Triangle or the depth of relationships of a Circle.

If the Squiggle is surrounded by others who have all the trappings of a conventional life, it can make them question if they have made the right choices. Of course, if given a choice, Squiggles would do the same thing all over again in a heartbeat because their greatest triumph is the sheer breadth of their life experiences.

The pure Squiggle has wanderlust and an unquenchable need to experiment, explore and discover. That can never be replaced. Yes, in later years, the Squiggle's aging body is not able to do as much, but you will still see those old eyes twinkle.

A 68-year-old Squiggle client wrote this on her social media, which explains what evolution means to people like her: 'Now I am older, I shall boldly wear mixed prints and stripes in purple, with a red hat that doesn't suit me ... And learn to spit. Who cares, as long as I have lived my life to the fullest!'

POSITIVE THINGS TO SAY
TO YOURSELF

■

BOX

I AM PERFECT JUST THE WAY I AM

I RELEASE MY NEED TO CONTROL THINGS

I TRUST EVERYONE IS DOING THE BEST THEY CAN FROM THEIR
AWARENESS

IT'S OKAY TO RELAX AND ENJOY MYSELF

IT'S OKAY TO MAKE MISTAKES AND LEARN FROM THEM

THE PAST IS OVER

I NOW FREE MYSELF FROM DESTRUCTIVE FEARS AND DOUBTS

I ENJOY TODAY AND CHEERFULLY LOOK FORWARD TO
TOMORROW

I ASK FOR WHAT I WANT AND NEED

LIFE BRINGS ME ONLY GOOD EXPERIENCES

I DESERVE THE BEST, AND I ACCEPT IT NOW

POSITIVE THINGS TO SAY
TO YOURSELF

▲

TRIANGLE

IT'S SAFE TO BE VULNERABLE

MY FEELINGS ARE AS VALUABLE AS MY ACCOMPLISHMENTS

I TAKE TIME TO RELAX AND GROW

I AM LOVED FOR WHO I AM. AND NOT WHAT I ACHIEVE

I AM WILLING TO SEE OTHERS AS EQUALS

I AM WILLING TO TRUST MORE

I RELEASE MY NEED TO CONTROL THE OUTCOME

I KNOW WHEN TO PUSH AND WHEN TO REST

I VALUE COLLABORATION OVER COMPETITION

I'M OPEN TO ACCEPT NEW PERSPECTIVES

I TRUST THAT EVERYONE IS DOING THE BEST THEY CAN FROM
THE AWARENESS THEY HAVE

POSITIVE THINGS TO SAY
TO YOURSELF

CIRCLE

MY NEEDS ARE AS IMPORTANT AS EVERYONE ELSE'S

I SPEAK UP FOR WHAT I WANT

I AM WORTHY OF RECIEVING LOVE

I AM PERFECT JUST THE WAY I AM

I LOVE AND APPROVE OF MYSELF

I DRAW BOUNDARIES WITH EASE AND COMPASSION

I AM GOOD ENOUGH

I HONOUR MY NEEDS AND FEELINGS

IT'S SAFE TO BE ME

I RELEASE ALL PAST HURT AND PAIN. I OPEN MYSELF UP TO

ABUNDANT LOVE AND POSSIBILTIES

ALL IS WELL

POSITIVE THINGS TO SAY
TO YOURSELF

SQUIGGLE

MY WELL-BEING IS MY TOP PRIORITY

I TAKE ADEQUATE REST TO RECHARGE MY BODY

THERE IS ENOUGH TIME FOR EVERYTHING

EVERYTHING I NEED COMES TO ME AT THE PERFECT TIME

IT IS SAFE TO LOOK WITHIN

I HAVE ENOUGH. THERE IS ENOUGH.

I AM DEEPLY FULFILLED BY ALL THAT I DO

I STAY IN THE PRESENT MOMENT AND ENJOY THE SMALL
THINGS

I BALANCE MY LIFE BETWEEN WORK, REST AND PLAY

I TRUST THE PROCESS OF LIFE

ALL IS WELL IN MY WORLD

POSITIVE THINGS TO SAY
TO YOURSELF

RECTANGLE

I TRUST THAT ALL MY QUESTIONS ARE ANSWERED AT THE RIGHT TIME

I LET GO OF ALL FEAR AND DOUBT, AND LIFE BECOMES SIMPLE AND EASY FOR ME

EVERYTHING I NEED COMES TO ME AT THE PERFECT TIME

I FEEL GLORIOUS, DYNAMIC ENERGY. I AM ACTIVE AND ALIVE

I AM A UNIQUE AND BEAUTIFUL SOUL

I TRUST MYSELF

I AM OPEN TO NEW AND WONDERFUL CHALLENGES

I FLOW EASILY WITH NEW EXPERIENCES, NEW CHALLENGES, AND NEW PEOPLE WHO ENTER MY LIFE

GOLDEN OPPORTUNITIES ARE EVERYWHERE FOR ME

AS I SAY YES TO LIFE, LIFE SAYS YES TO ME

I AM GUIDED AND PROTECTED AT ALL TIMES

ALL IS WELL IN MY WORLD

A Final Note

Dear Sneha,
I attended your Psycho-Geometrics workshop yesterday. It came to me at the perfect time, and I now understand what is going wrong in my life.

I work hard, and I am a people-pleaser—a Box–Circle in the Psycho-Geometrics language. These qualities have helped me achieve a certain level of success and now I am a manager in a fast-paced, high-pressure service business. On the personal front, I have been able to create some measure of security and stability for my family, which means a lot to me.

My problem is that I have created a monster in my boss. She is so used to my structure and my organised approach that she pretty much expects me to deliver perfectly all the time now—which, of course, is highly stressful for me.

Any tiny lapse gets a nasty comment from her. Here's an example: she asked me for a report and gave me the deadline. I don't usually miss deadlines, but I was travelling that day. My five-hour flight was delayed, so I sent the report as soon as I landed. I was already swamped with work (I can't seem to say no or delegate effectively).

To my mind, I met the deadline as best as I possibly could, despite the constraints. I hoped to hear, 'It's great you got it done despite the challenges.' Instead, her response was: 'How do I get you to submit your work before the deadline?'

Even at home, I am doing my best, yet there is always more expected of me. I don't feel respected or valued enough. This is driving me crazy. I know I need to reduce my Box traits, but how do I do it?

Regards,

Troubled Box–Circle

I often get asked, 'How can one reduce the dominance of a shape?' Circles want to be less Circle-like when they get hurt, Boxes want to be less Box-like when people take their dependability for granted, Squiggles want to be less Squiggle-like when their dreams don't come true and Triangles want to be less Triangle-like when they lose their family and health along the way.

According to the science of shapes, rather than focusing your energy on minimising the existence of your dominant shape (because that is akin to swimming against the tide), you need to focus on enhancing the presence of the other shapes within you, so that it creates more balance. But why does the imbalance happen in the first place?

Our dominant shape develops in response to the demands of the environment around us. My Circle traits of being loving, nurturing, polite and pleasing got me acceptance and validation. While it worked at a certain stage of my life, the continued dominance of the Circle deprived me of the strengths of the other shapes. The real challenge was to get in touch with my least used shapes—the Triangle and the Squiggle—and bring them to the fore.

The fact is that we humans seek balance in our lives. We have a natural tendency to move towards homeostasis, a stable internal environment. The Box needs the flexibility of a Squiggle. The Triangle needs the sensitivity of a Circle. The Squiggle needs the objectivity of a Box. The Circle needs the boundaries of a Triangle. All shapes are interdependent and of equal value. The healthiest personality is the one that can integrate all shapes within and can bring to the fore different aspects of their personality depending on the situation. This allows you to not get stuck within the rigid outlines of a dominant shape and experience the magnificence of each one, which in turn allows you to be the best version of yourself.

Here is an amazing secret to create the healthiest version of you. Follow these five steps:

Step 1: Recognise that all five shapes exist within you.

Step 2: Identify which shape or shapes are dominant and which are least used, and how they impact your life and your relationships.

Step 3: Accept your dominant shape or shapes, but do not use them as an excuse for your poor behaviour.

Step 4: Embrace your weaker or lesser used shapes. These embody the qualities you need to now develop to evolve.

Step 5: Don't resist the Rectangle within you. Remember that the Rectangle is the passageway to change.

While the book ends here, your journey of discovery, acceptance, compassion and awareness begins now. Psycho-Geometrics® is a wonderful gift—a gift of a fuller understanding of yourself and the changes you experience from time to time. It's a tool that will help you understand the inner worlds of the people around you.

This information will change the way you interact with others. It will help you walk the path of growth and expansion. Use it as and when you need to improve your relationships. Live it, share it, discuss it and allow it to become an integral part of your life. This information will immensely benefit you and those you value in your life.

As Dr Susan Dellinger says, just remember to celebrate ALL the shapes within you.

> Box your Boss!
>
> Circle your Peers!
>
> Triangle your Juniors!
>
> Squiggle your Lover!
>
> And Rectangle Yourself!
>
> Always be open to growth and change.

Acknowledgements

This book is a result of many magnificent people who have touched my life in ways that enriched me and nudged me to grow. If I had to write each person's name, I would have to write a whole chapter! I apologise if I don't name you all, but you know you mean the world to me. Thank you for making this possible.

Dr Susan Dellinger, a huge thank you for building the outstanding Psycho-Geometrics® system. You have changed millions of lives with your work, and I am fortunate to have met you. Your vibrance, passion, generosity and joie de vivre are infectious. You inspired me to write this book.

A special thanks to all my clients. I have gained so much because you have trusted me with your life stories and shared your personal journey with me. I am a better person because of you. Thank you to tens of thousands of ISRA participants who have attended our workshops and become a part of our ever-growing community.

A big thank you to the ISRA team for sharing my dream to make a difference in the world. You make it possible for us to grow.

Heartfelt gratitude to my family for being an incredible support system. I hope you know how much I love you and cherish you. My father, my hero, you deserve a special mention because you would have been proud to see this book. I miss you every day.

To my parents by marriage, you have been my cheerleaders as I wrote every page. Your constant loving encouragement gave me the impetus to keep writing. Thank you for being so wonderful.

Toral, your support, love and guidance have been incredible. Thank you for always standing by my side and holding me in the warmth of your circle. I owe this one to you.

Special thanks to the extraordinary people who got trained as Psycho-Geometrics® Facilitators. Your work is making a difference in the world. You make us proud.

Thank you to my closest friends who reviewed the manuscript and motivated me to keep going. Special thanks to Dr Patricia J. Crane, Rick Nichols, Ralph H. Kilmann, Lucia Giovannini, Sinisa Ubovic, Aylin Algun, Fernando Niño and Ivana Tomic for taking the time to write insightful reviews. It heightened my belief in the book.

Thank you to my outstanding teachers, my incredible friends, the Heal Your Life® tribe and all those who have touched my life with their presence. You have been a huge part of my healing journey. I feel blessed to have you.

A special thanks to Karthika, my publisher at Westland Books, for believing in this book. You have been the midwife who helped me birth this book. I will forever be grateful. The whole team at Westland, you are incredible. Thank you for supporting the project with your heart.

Finally, I thank you, my readers, for being open and willing to go on this journey. I truly wish for you to lead happier and more fulfilled lives, and I hope this book takes you one step forward in that direction. Because you deserve it!

Want to Be a Part of Our Tribe?

I really hope you enjoyed *What Shape Are You?* This book is a culmination of all my experiences as a psychologist and as the founder of ISRA.

To tell you a little more, my partner Shashank and I founded our company ISRA in 2007. We are passionate entrepreneurs with a common mission of making the world a happier place to live in.

We have strived to create mentally and emotionally healthy individuals, families and organisations. We have built a large community of like-minded growth-driven people, whom we affectionately call the 'ISRA Tribe'. We constantly offer webinars and workshops to our participants, which contribute tremendously to their growth and well-being.

We have spent more than a decade teaching people skills which help them become better individuals, thrive in their relationships and succeed at their workplace. Our strength lies in using psychological frameworks to create lasting positive change. Over the years, our presence has expanded globally, and we have impacted over 75,000 lives, in over ten countries and across over 50 MNCs.

If you would like to be a part of our ever-growing tribe, do write to us at info@isra.co.in.

Apart from this, you will also find many more courses and webinars on resilience, assertive communication, conflict management, leadership skills and a host of other subjects on our website: www.isra.co.in.

ISRA also specialises in corporate training workshops with an impressive list of multinational clients across ten countries. Want to organise a workshop for your company? You can connect with us on info@isra.co.in.

Learn More About Psycho-Geometrics®

Psycho-Geometrics® (the framework on which this book is based) has literally transformed millions of lives globally. It's a new language that can help you make better friends and deeper connections and thrive in any environment.

We have more resources to help you understand and use this tool to great effect in your personal and professional lives. This is the path you can take to go deeper in your journey with Psycho-Geometrics®.

Assessment

You can take the Psycho-Geometrics® assessment and get a detailed personalised report with your scores and analysis. Readers can use code 'WSAY' to avail 20 per cent discount.

Visit: www.whatshapeareyou.com

Online Masterclass

To learn more about the shapes, I have created an online masterclass which gives you access to my learning videos and PDF downloads. This is a self-paced online course on Psycho-Geometrics® in which you have access to:

- 24 Pre-recorded Videos
- 12 Reflection Worksheets (PDF)
- 26 Topics
- Information Downloads

Register here: www.whatshapeareyou.com

Readers can use code 'WSAY' to avail 20 per cent discount.

What Shape Are You? Psycho-Geometrics® Certification

Do you want to start teaching workshops based on the Psycho-Geometrics® system? Attend our official six-day online certification which certifies you to lead workshops based on the Psycho-Geometrics® framework. You receive a detailed manual with exercises, to facilitate your own workshops.

Visit: www.whatshapeareyou.com

Psycho-Geometrics® is copyrighted material and cannot be used for training purposes without certification and official licensing. ISRA is the sole owner of the system in India, with exclusive rights.